The Future
in the
Making

Dyckman W. Vermilye, EDITOR

1973

CURRENT ISSUES IN HIGHER EDUCATION

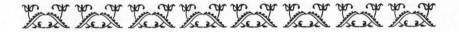

ASSOCIATE EDITOR, *Joseph Axelrod*

THE FUTURE
IN THE
MAKING

 Jossey-Bass Publishers

San Francisco • Washington • London • 1973

THE FUTURE IN THE MAKING
Dyckman W. Vermilye, Editor

THE JOSSEY-BASS SERIES IN HIGHER EDUCATION

 A publication of the

AMERICAN ASSOCIATION FOR HIGHER EDUCATION
National Center for Higher Education
One Dupont Circle, Northwest
Washington, D.C. 20036

DYCKMAN W. VERMILYE, *Executive Director*

The American Association for Higher Education, AAHE,
promotes higher education and provides a national
voice for individual members. AAHE, founded in 1870,
is the only national higher education organization
open to faculty members, administrators, graduate
students, and trustees without regard to rank, discipline,
or type or size of institution. AAHE is dedicated to
the professional development of college and university
educators, to the achievement of their educational
objectives, and to the improvement of conditions
of service.

Preface

P robably at no time in history has a society concerned itself so much with the future as ours has, but the future keeps surprising us. Sometimes the surprise is a pleasant one, like an unexpected cure for a dread disease, and sometimes not so pleasant, like the discovery that some of our cures have caused diseases worse than the ones they got rid of. To a great extent, our state of future shock results from our failure to take account of the phenomenon of exponential growth— the periodic doubling of an existing quantity. For most of us, exponential growth is associated with the population problem. Demographers have used it for some time to scare the hell out of us. But a corresponding phenomenon seems to be operating in the less quantitative aspects of contemporary life: technology, the arts, fashion, life styles, even individual expectations. Here, too, the accelerating rate of change confuses efforts to figure out the shape of tomorrow.

But even though we cannot figure out the precise shape, we are getting a general picture of alternative futures, and that picture suggests some general, but urgent, courses of action. We need to know more, but the need to act now on what we already know seems far more critical. What holds us back? Perhaps the greatest obstacle is that such problems don't impress us really graphically until it is too late to deal with them. The classic illustration of a false sense of security is the example of lily pads growing in a large pond. If a pond had a single lily pad, and the number of lily pads doubled each day, it would take quite some time for the pond to be half covered by the plants. However, at that point it would take only one day for the entire pond to be covered. If the owner of the pond wanted to keep it from being choked by the lily pads but could clear out only an eighth of the surface area each day, he would have procrastinated beyond the point of controlling the problem.

Some scholars of the human predicament—and not just alarmists—believe we may soon approach that point ourselves. Their warnings against the heretofore prevailing philosophy of open-ended growth and expansion are beginning to be taken seriously. Terms like *steady state, no-growth,* and *equilibrium* are entering the vernacular of economics, industry, and politics. Birth rates show signs of leveling off. Oil companies are asking people to drive slower to save fuel. Congress is talking about limiting automobile horsepower. Amid controversy, nuclear power plants are springing up across the country to meet energy demands as other sources of energy give out. People are getting concerned. If there has been nothing definitive yet in the way of action, at any rate the stage is set.

What has higher education to do with all this? Everything. Institutions—long proponents of the growth ethic—have been victims of it along with everyone else. Having fed and been fed by the Gross National Product, they have been called on to make a new accounting of themselves—both for the way they do business and for the business they do. Some, in the interest of survival, are learning to conduct their affairs in a steady-state manner. But how many are meeting the larger challenge, that of preparing students to live responsibly and well in a steady-state world?

As in past years, this book is about a wide range of current issues in higher education. Not all of them bear directly on the growing responsibility of higher education to ensure and enhance the quality of life. But each chapter can be—and will be, I hope—read in that context. There is, I believe, evidence throughout the book of a new sensitivity, a new kind of thinking that puts quality before quantity, moderation before excess, better before bigger. And in some chapters— notably the contribution of Lewis Perelman and Dennis Meadows—the new thinking is as explicit as an invitation to go clear out the pond.

My thanks to Martin Lichterman, who served as chairman of the Twenty-Eighth National Conference on Higher Education, and to the other members of his planning committee, for it was their suggestions and recommendations that led to the sessions which generated these papers.

Washington, D.C.   DYCKMAN W. VERMILYE
September 1973

Contents

Contributors

ROBERT C. ANDRINGA, minority staff director, House Committee on Education and Labor, U.S. House of Representatives

ALISON R. BERNSTEIN, assistant to the president, Staten Island Community College

EDWARD J. BLOUSTEIN, president, Rutgers

ERNEST L. BOYER, chancellor, State University of New York, Albany

JOSEPH P. COSAND, director, Center for the Study of Higher Education, University of Michigan; formerly deputy commissioner for higher education, U.S. Office of Education

K. PATRICIA CROSS, senior research psychologist, Educational Testing Service, and research educator, Center for Research and Development in Higher Education, University of California, Berkeley

ROBERT M. DIAMOND, assistant vice chancellor, Center for Instructional Development, Syracuse University

GEORGE P. DOHERTY, president, Bell and Howell Schools, Inc., Chicago

KENNETH E. EBLE, professor of English, University of Utah; formerly director, Project to Improve College Teaching

EUGENE H. FRAM, professor of marketing and director, Center for Management Study, Rochester Institute of Technology

ROGER W. HEYNS, president, American Council on Education

JOHN W. HICKS, assistant to the president, Purdue University

JACK H. JONES, president, Jones College

CHARLES V. KIDD, executive secretary, Association of American Universities

FRANCIS P. KOSTER, doctoral candidate in the Program for the Study of the Future in Education, School of Education, University of Massachusetts, Amherst; formerly ombudsman, C. W. Post College

HUGH W. LANE, president, National Scholarship Service and Fund for Negro Students

DENNIS L. MEADOWS, director, Club of Rome Project on the Predicament of Mankind

LEWIS PERELMAN, Graduate School of Education, Harvard University

ALBERT H. QUIE, member, U.S. House of Representatives

EDWARD JOSEPH SHOBEN, JR., associate provost for graduate education and research, University of Pittsburgh; formerly executive vice-president, Evergreen State College

WILLIAM F. STURNER, assistant president, Oakland University

JOHN WILLIAM WARD, president, Amherst

VALENTINE ROSSILLI WINSEY, associate professor (adjunct), Behavioral Sciences, John Jay College, CUNY

The Future
in the
Making

PART ONE

Democracy in Action

If we were to name the events that have had the greatest impact on the American mind during the third quarter of the present century, surely three of those events would be the launching of Sputnik, the war in Southeast Asia, and—the major event of 1973—the Watergate scandal. Every future historian who analyzes the developing patterns of American thought during this period will need to explain how Watergate could have happened in America.

It is inevitable that any yearbook published in 1973, if it adequately performs its function, should reflect back to the reader this Event of the Year, if only in indirect ways. It is interesting, but perhaps not too surprising, then, that the chapters of this volume should present us with the two major messages of Watergate—even though the essays were all prepared early in 1973, before the impact of the scandal had begun to be felt. These messages are particularly apparent in the essays of Parts One and Two, which deal with the political and economic forces that are now shaping the future of American *higher education. For Watergate symbolizes two fundamental principles that are expressed in a variety of ways in these essays. The first of these is illustrated in Part One, while the second is also the concern of the essays of Part Two and is discussed in the headnote for that section of the book.*

The first principle relates to the concept of political power, and it emphasizes the enormous influence—on our entire society—of the ethical and political views of certain individual men and women. This principle asserts that, although impersonal forces which exist within our societal pattern have a strong impact on us, regardless of the decisions of individual men, a great deal of what occurs in our daily lives nonetheless results directly from the decisions of specific individuals—namely, those who hold political power. This is why the abuse of political power in a society such as ours is so dangerous to our welfare.

Applied to the field of higher education, this principle can be translated simply: the decision-making mechanisms affecting the future of higher education in the United States are primarily political in nature. The significance of this principle has become increasingly evident in recent years. The sooner all educators—administrators, researchers, and teaching faculty alike—recognize this truth, the more effectively will they be able to help shape the future of the colleges and universities they serve. Albert H. Quie, Robert C. Andringa, John W. Hicks, and Francis P. Koster cogently demonstrate this thesis in the four essays of Part One.

JOSEPH AXELROD

The View from the Hill

Albert H. Quie

Members of the higher education community are probably well aware of the criticism Congress has leveled at higher education in recent months. The criticism comes mainly from members of Congress who were most involved in the three-year consideration of the Education Amendments of 1972, signed into law last June. We found that there was very little discussion within the higher education community about the legislation. The few who communicated with Congress provided us too little information, and when they did it was not at the time we needed it most. One key member of our Education and Labor Committee with close ties to many universities has said publicly that he was absolutely embarrassed by the scope and quality of information provided by the higher education community. It seemed to me the major educational associations chose to concentrate on the politics of

3

getting one particular formula for institutional aid adopted, while leaving most of the necessary data-gathering and analytical work to the Congress.

Even now, when so many people in higher education recognize how ineffectual they were with the Congress, in dealing with the problems of the last two years, I do not believe that sufficient efforts are being made to remedy this lack of communication. Of all the people who come to my office to talk with me about the innumerable issues that I am directly involved with on the Education and Labor Committee, or about problems of my congressional district, there is rarely anyone from higher education who comes in to discuss either what is happening on the campuses or his views on proposals for administering the Higher Education Amendments of 1972.

It isn't that nobody comes. In recent months I have been approached by representatives of associations who had virtually ignored most members of our committee and the similar committee in the Senate for the last two years. They are now attempting to make amends. Most of them approach me about a bread and butter problem of some funds being cut back. There is one man from the State of Minnesota who keeps in very close touch either on the telephone or in person, and that is Chancellor Mitau of the State College System.

I feel the need for conversation with administrators, faculty members, students, and trustees in order to adequately perform my duties. As the ranking member of the Education and Labor Committee who through the last fifteen years has had as strong an interest in higher education problems as anyone in the Congress, I often have had to seek out educators in order to meet with them.

Now, let me compare the higher education community in this regard with three other groups. The Chambers of Commerce from various cities in my district often invite me to be with them at early morning breakfasts to talk over problems of mutual interest. Farmer groups do the same thing. Sometimes the National Farmers Organization, Farm Bureau, and Farmers Union members meet together with me so I can listen to their differing views and learn by the interchange. And every year the Building and Construction Trades officials come out to Washington for a breakfast. I have missed only one such breakfast in the last fifteen years.

I have a feeling the higher education community is like the fellow who says to his friend, "Why don't you come over and visit with me sometime?" when he knows that the friend is so busy he doesn't have time to do it. If you really want to get together with a friend to talk to him about something, you have to make a firm invitation, advising him of the date and making special arrangements.

Although I personally feel that people in higher education should be concerned about past performance, my own greater concern is that we discover together new ways to improve the quality of public decision-making about postsecondary education in the future. While our campuses provide one of the nation's greatest resources for knowledge and insight into a multitude of social problems, the higher education community seems to put a low priority on developing knowledge and insight about itself. The impression left to some observers is that the academic community expects as a matter of right to be supported in its pursuit of its own goals. Although many academic leaders are now beginning to point out that such unquestioning support from the public has, at least temporarily, run out, their cries for attention seem to be greeted with more apathy than concern by most faculty and students. In a day when even private colleges are dependent on public subsidies, it is imperative that a much larger segment of the higher education community turn its attention and resources in the days ahead to the major questions of postsecondary education policy.

I am struck by the in-depth studies some of the other organizations provide to the Congress. Farmer groups, Chambers of Commerce, and organized labor, again pointing to those three, will provide in-depth economic studies for us if we ask them. Interestingly enough, some of them must turn to institutions of higher education to find the expertise for such studies. The higher education community needs to provide such information and learn to draw the attention of Congress to it. The higher education community needs to participate, more than it has in the past, in the great tradition of Americans petitioning their elected representatives. It must look candidly at the art of lobbying in its broadest sense. If the term *lobbying* brings negative associations to mind, then we must reconsider the bases for those associations.

Lobbying, in the sense that I use it here, is the process of providing timely and relevant information to legislators so that they can make the very best decisions in the public interest. It is an absolutely vital function if our form of government is to operate as it should. The public is not endangered by vigorous, effective, legal, and ethical lobbying. The public is endangered only when it elects an official who becomes captive to any one lobby group, or one who becomes lazy in sorting out the public interest from the lobbyist's interests. Some activities of some lobbies do run counter to sound ethical principles, but the popular press has left a distorted picture of Washington lobbyists. Most that I know operate completely above board and serve as the vital link between those who make the law and those who are most affected by it. If there is one aspect of the activities of the higher education lobby that deserves the highest marks, it is ethics. In fact, some politicians might say educators are so above board that they come across as unbelievably naive. I hesitate to be the judge of that. At any rate, higher education is not losing the public's confidence due to unethical lobbying tactics.

The major constraint on the higher education lobby is a vague but tough legal boundary line. Most colleges and univeresities and almost all higher education associations are among some 175,000 "charitable organizations" registered under Section 501(c)(3) of the Internal Revenue Code. This status exempts them from paying income taxes and allows them to receive tax deductible donations. It also allows them to receive grants from foundations and government agencies. In order to qualify for this tax exemption and to be eligible for contributions, a 501(c)(3) organization must comply with certain limitations. In part, the law says with respect to these exempt organizations, "no *substantial part* of the *activities* of which is carrying on propaganda, or otherwise attempting, to influence *legislation,* and which does not participate in, or intervene in (including the publishing or distributing of statements), *any* political campaign on behalf of *any* candidate for public office." The vexing problem is the lack of a clear definition of what is meant by "no substantial part of the activities." A rough rule of thumb, I understand, is that a 501(c)(3) organization *might* be safe so long as no more than 5 percent of its annual expenditures is spent on lobbying activities. But the IRS looks at the nature of lobbying activity, not just at the amount of money spent on it. It is clear that 501(c)(3) organizations are prohibited from *any* participation in political campaigns.

According to testimony given last year by Edwin S. Cohen, then Assistant Secretary of the Treasury for Tax Policy, the phrase "carrying on propaganda, or otherwise attempting to influence legislation" has been interpreted by the IRS to permit the publication of studies that may become the subject of legislation. The 501(c)(3) language has also been interpreted to allow associations to attempt to influence executive branch decisions relating to the application and administration of legislation. There have been and are now legislative proposals to clarify this provision of the tax laws. The Administration has agreed to the need for more specific legislation, and many members of Congress agree, but there is as yet no consensus on the specific changes which would be in the public interest.

Presently, what may be done in Washington? First, any tax exempt organization is free to provide information at the request of a committee of Congress or of a member of Congress. I believe most officials of educational associations know that they have a standing invitation to provide me or our Committee any data or reports that would be of help to us. Second, any college administrator, faculty member, or student is free to contact his or her representative in the legislature without jeopardizing anyone's tax status. That is why people in higher education are urged by their associations in Washington to communicate with their Senators or Representatives about legislative proposals. Therefore, when legislation is being discussed in our Committee, I am sure the calls go out, particularly to key "constituents" of Committee members. Thus, because of the tax laws, individual educators can play a more active role in supporting or opposing legislation than some associations feel able to do. And a well-documented letter from an individual—especially an individual who is known and respected by the Congressman receiving the letter—can have a considerable amount of influence.

Associations organize their activities in support of specific legislation with considerable care and always with the tax laws in mind. The IRS Code restricts any association from major, all-out efforts. There is always that haunting possibility of having to prove to some IRS examiner that "no substantial part" of the association's activity was related to influencing legislation. So most of the work is done by word of mouth—by phone calls, telegrams, and personal visits. While these legal constraints put real limits on official organizational lobby campaigns, I believe there have to be some reasonable boundaries on this kind of activity by organizations that want preferential tax treatment. No organization can have it both ways. The National Education Association recently gave up its tax exempt status in order to participate in active lobbying and political campaigns. It has the tax status of a trade association, and judgments vary as to the impact of its rather recent decision to change its status.

There is one final legal factor to consider, but it is far less important than the tax laws. In 1946, Congress passed the Federal Registration of Lobbying Act which Assistant Secretary Cohen said in his testimony is "about as vague a piece of legislation as was ever written." Some ten thousand individuals and organizations are registered with the Clerk of the House of Representatives as official lobbyists under this Act. The definitions are so vague and the enforcement procedures so inadequate, however, that this law does not provide meaningful information about, or regulation of, Washington lobbyists. Registration is almost voluntary, depending to a great extent on how an organization determines what portion of its activity is lobbying under the definitions of this law. So far as I know, the vast majority of higher education associations do not register under this Act. A check with a recent listing of registered lobbyists showed only the following higher education organizations: American Association of Presidents of Independent Colleges and Universities, College Placement Council, Inc., Association of American Law Schools, National Student Lobby, Full Funding of Education Programs.

Within this legal framework, just who does communicate with Congress about higher education? Very few people—I would guess no more than eight or ten—consider one of their major tasks to be regular liaison with the Congress on matters of postsecondary education. Almost all of these individuals are paid staff members of Washington-based national higher education associations. They are specialists who grow to understand the legislative process, making it a priority to meet regularly with congressmen and committee staff, and studying the complex provisions of the many annual legislative proposals. They have their own mechanisms for sharing information and developing a coordinated strategy among their individual organizations. I believe this approach to congressional communications will always be necessary. The complexity of legislation, the importance of being available to Congress on short notice, the limited time people on the Hill have to meet personally with higher education representatives, and the fact that educational leaders have many other things to accomplish than to constantly monitor federal legislation—all of these things point to the need for some professional federal relations people in Washington.

As federal involvement in higher education increases, state boards of higher education, regional and state associations of institutions, and even large universities are beginning to hire their own Washington representatives. Many of these people spend a major portion of their time keeping track of the red tape emanating from the executive branch. But several of them also keep an eye on the activities of Congress. We meet from time to time with many of these Washington representatives. They can be very helpful and they provide the Congress with useful feedback on how various proposals would affect the individual universities or the systems of institutions they represent. Although some congressmen assume that each of these Washington-based educators speaks for a broad segment of higher education, I am more inclined to accept the data supplied by each of these educators as valuable information from *one* knowledgeable person—who, I hope, bases his opinions on frequent feedback from the institutions he represents. Usually, however, these communications seem to be based on a sample of no more than a dozen or so conversations with individual campus leaders.

There are weaknesses also in relying too heavily on the Washington-based educational associations. First, they do not generate enough information. Second, communications from these associations do not constitute a balanced picture. Ninety percent of the input from national associations reflects the ideas of college presidents. We do not need less knowledge of their views; we need more. But we also need the judgments of faculty and trustees. Their input is almost nil. It is a mystery to me why more associations representing the academic disciplines do not comment on major legislation that deeply affects the lives of faculty members. And until the last year or so we almost never heard from students. Now they are beginning to get organized to make their views known. That is an encouraging sign to us.

Another problem of the organized higher education lobbyists is their natural desire to present a "unified front" to the Congress. Indeed, many individual congressmen ask the education associations how the Congress is to make policy decisions on higher education legislation when the major associations cannot even agree. It puts the associations in a difficult position. I am one who expects the associations to work together on major policy questions, but I do not expect, for example, that the Association of American Universities will agree with the American Association of Junior and Community Colleges on every issue. Of the dozens of federal programs, some definitely help one type of institution more than another. We want to understand those differences so the Congress, and not some small group located at One Dupont Circle, in Washington, D.C., can decide what is good public policy.

Perhaps even more important than the efforts of associations is what happens between individual congressmen and their constituents back home. Like any human being, a congressman is often influenced more by his personal experiences than by what he might read in an academic journal, or indeed, in an association policy statement. This more direct form of communication is not geared to specific legislation, it does not require much expertise, and it is best done on the campus itself. There are many exciting developments in postsecondary education today which are unknown to many congressmen. I would urge that each campus community share these things with its own congressmen at every opportunity. We enjoy interacting with students and faculty on the campus and we want to see new programs. Too often, however, the sponsoring campus group rushes a congressman to an auditorium, lets him give a speech, rushes him to a press conference, and perhaps to a quick stop in the president's office, and right out to the airport again. That kind of scheduling wastes a good opportunity to educate a congressman about what is happening. Without frequent contact with the campuses, too many congressmen not serving on the Education Committee have to rely mostly on their own or their children's educational experiences.

I would like to note briefly some of the unique aspects of communicating to Congress about appropriations. It is the nature of every interest group in the country to muster great efforts at budget time. I can only say that there is no way for the Congress to appropriate money for all that it has authorized in education, health, housing, the environment, welfare, manpower, and countless other deserving social programs. This incident will serve as an example of the false hopes the Congress has held out: I was talking with Health, Education and Welfare Secretary Eliot Richardson at the beginning of the year just before he transferred from HEW to the Department of Defense. He said that when he left office in HEW at the end of the Eisenhower administration, appropriations for the Department were two-hundred million under authorization; four years ago when he came into the Nixon administration, appropriations were six billion dollars below authorization; when he left to go to the Defense Department at the beginning of this year, appropriations were twelve billion dollars below authorization. These are the false hopes that Congress has raised, giving people the impression that if it were not for a "hard-hearted" administration, all their desires could be met. Appropriations have not decreased nor have they stayed the same. HEW appropriations for the last fiscal year were seventy-five billion dollars; this year they were eighty-six billion, and the President himself proposes in his budget, despite the cutbacks we have heard about, one hundred and two billion for the next fiscal year. The President proposed a federal budget for this fiscal year of $248 billion. He indicated to the Congress that he definitely wanted the budget to stay at $250 billion. However, just before the Congress left for home in October 1972, it increased appropriations for this fiscal year up to $261 billion. For the coming fiscal year, the President asked that we stay within a $269 billion budget. Some hard decisions must be made. Congress must find better ways to deal more responsibly with the budget problem. I hope that proposals now being developed to restructure congressional decision-making procedures in the budget area will prove workable. But I am convinced we will never provide the federal money that Congress recognizes is needed for education unless the Congress does exactly what the Office of Management and Budget is now doing, and that is to set a total limit on spending and then set a total limit on each of the approximately fifteen separate appropriation bills. Congress must decide its own priorities, and then require a two-thirds vote to raise the appropriation in any particular area above the limit set. If such increases are made, Congress must assume the responsibility of either increasing taxes to pay for them, or of increasing the federal debt again. When President Nixon took office the federal debt was $358,790,157,000; in the spring of 1973 it was $452,821,020,000.

From the point of view of higher education, one must also be willing to make hard judgments about programs which might be outdated or whose objectives have been met. Full-funding is simply out of the question. Indeed, with over one hundred federal education programs, some will not get funded at all. Educators can help the Congress by showing their representatives what impact the budget would have on their own institutions. We get a very considerable amount of information about the national picture; too seldom do we understand the effect of the budget from the consumer's perspective. Congress also needs to know which programs have priority over others from the vantage point of the campus. This kind of candid feedback is something that association officials in Washington find it very difficult to give.

Since so much of America's intelligentsia is concentrated in our colleges and universities, it seems that Congress should be able to receive from these scholars studies indicating where programs can be cut as well as where increases are needed. Also, Congress needs a determination of where taxes may need to be increased and, if they are, what kind of taxes they ought to be. This approach certainly would demonstrate a sense of responsibility in making requests for federal funds in the future.

The opportunity I have had in this paper to turn from the substance of federal legislation to a consideration of the political process—specifically the communication of the views of the higher education community to Congress—has been refreshing for me. As a congressman, I believe that as educators work together with the Congress to understand and improve this process, the quality of our laws will improve as well.

2

Congressional Staff
and Higher
Education Policy

Robert C. Andringa

🎕🎕🎕🎕🎕🎕🎕🎕

A great deal of misunderstanding exists about the political process—about the role of Congress in American education. Not only are many learned educators vague about the function of individual congressmen and committees in shaping legislation, they normally plead complete ignorance about the role of a committee staffer. Therefore, I would like to remove some of the shrouds of secrecy about the staff role and share some observations about our communications with the postsecondary community. I do so with the hope that many more members of that community will be motivated to become involved in this complex but exciting process.

Certainly communication is a key component of the formula for good legislation. As Mr. Quie points out in the preceding essay, an important part of his communication takes place outside of Washington as well as in his Capitol Hill office. As a member of his committee staff, I often join him in the latter setting. Staff members share many experiences with congressmen—in hearings, in informal briefing sessions, in meetings with administration officials, in staff meetings, and on untold other occasions when the many wheels of the political process are in gear. But the committee staff is also expected to maintain a whole range of tasks while the congressmen on the committee are engaged in carrying out their seemingly unlimited activities that are apart from education legislation.

Before I attempt an overview of what the staff role is, I would like first to deflate one of the myths that many carry over from high school civics. I speak of often used phrases such as "our association contacted the Congress about this matter." Or, "we made our views known to Congress about that problem." When referring to legislation that gets signed into law, the press often refers to a specific provision as something "Congress decided." And many of the Washington representatives of the higher education community, administration officials, and others often argue a point by stating that "Congress intended that it be done this way." Now, in one sense there is nothing wrong with making these statements. But do not be misled by the use of the word *Congress* in the generic sense. Congress operates mainly through the committee system. In the House, we have roughly 120 standing authorizing committees which shape legislation in fairly well-defined areas. Except on major national issues, lobbyists aim their efforts at the particular committee or committees having jurisdiction over their area of interest. Legislation is developed mainly in subcommittee and full-committee meetings. Once a bill leaves a committee, it becomes much more difficult to change. So on the majority of issues, when someone says "It was the intent of Congress," it most likely means that it was the intent of a small group of members of the committee (or even one member) who developed that particular provision of law. As the senior Republican in the House who negotiates the final stages of education legislation, Mr. Quie is constantly being asked to interpret "congressional intent" whenever opposing views emerge on a specific provision of law. Obviously, a staff member spends many hours in many places trying to define this elusive wisdom called congressional intent.

Some descriptive data might give you a sense of the growing fraternity of congressional staff. Each member of the House of Representatives is allowed to hire up to sixteen people for his personal staff. Senators have a somewhat larger office staff, depending on their salary allotment, which is determined by the population of their state. Especially on the House side, these people do not get too involved in the details of the legislation their boss is working on in committee. Rather, they help serve the members' constituents and keep their boss aware of the issues he will be asked to vote on, but which do not originate in his committee.

Those of us on committee staffs are of a somewhat different breed. Individuals on the staff tend to be more specialized. We must learn how to respond to requests from many congressmen who often hold opposing views. Like the office staffs of individual members of the House, however, we are not part of the Civil Service and so our jobs depend on how well we adjust and how much we contribute to the work of the several members on the committee. The advantage of this system is that members of the House have flexibility to hire the number and kind of people they feel are necessary at any given time.

Generally, the size of a committee staff is determined by the committee budget approved by the full House, the physical space available, and the desires of the members who do the hiring. The Education and Labor Committee has some sixty staff members hired by the Democrats, including the staffs of our eight subcommittees. The chairman of the full committee with the eight subcommittee chairmen hires and directs the work of these people. The Minority staff this year will probably not exceed fifteen. We are hired by Mr. Quie and spend most of our time with him and eight ranking members of the subcommittee. In all the House committees, there are approximately 550 professional staff people—a small group compared to the thousands in the executive branch, but I think a very competent group overall. They are recruited from many segments of society, perhaps half of them with legal backgrounds. Salaries for committee professional staff range from approximately $12,000 per year to a maximum of $36,000.

As I mentioned, each committee staff person tends to specialize. Most of my time is relegated to postsecondary education. Except when major postsecondary legislation is actively moving through the legislative mill, there are perhaps only four or five committee staff people in the entire Congress who spend half or more of their time keeping abreast of the federal role in postsecondary education. Fortunately, not many education issues are partisan in nature, so the Majority and Minority staffs often work closely together.

Here, then, in rapid-fire order, is a list of those things that make my life interesting. Allowing for certain differences in style, these examples are quite typical of other professional staff members in the education area as well. We do such things as:

Prepare background for and attend committee hearings;

Follow up information gained through the testimony of witnesses at hearings;

Draft legislation and amendments to legislation during various stages of the legislative process;

Meet with college presidents, student aid officers, state education officials, researchers, representatives of state and national associations and other individuals who find their way into our office;

Attend numerous meetings and seminars in Washington to discuss education problems, pending legislation and current law;

Attempt to keep abreast of the major journals, research studies, program reports and regulations, association news bulletins, and numerous Congressional publications;

Arrange special briefings to inform other Hill staff or Members about current issues and pending legislation;

Maintain correspondence with selected scholars and administrators around the country;

Consult with Congressmen about speeches, legislative ideas, journal articles, constituent problems, radio and television shows;

Serve on occasional commissions, task forces and advisory groups;

Keep one eye on the Senate at all times to make sure the House is never caught off guard;

Speak to visiting school children, college students, and other groups visiting Capitol Hill;

Attend local and out-of-town conferences on postsecondary education;

Visit, whenever possible, schools and colleges to see firsthand how federal programs are working;

Get briefed by, consult with, and keep tabs on the Office of Education and other executive agencies;

Answer phone inquiries until both ears are numb.

When I first drafted this list, even I was impressed by the diversity of our work. Then I immediately thought about the additional pages it would take to list the many hats a congressman wears. Some days one simply has to marvel that Congress gets as much accomplished as it does!

Any association attempting to monitor all legislation affecting higher education now has to keep an eye on at least five House committees: Interstate and Foreign Commerce for health legislation; Science and Astronautics for National Science Foundation and other science related programs; Veterans Affairs for veterans benefits; Ways and Means for tax legislation; and, of course, our committee for the Higher Education Act and other postsecondary education programs.

At the beginning of this Congress, a House Select Committee on Committees was formed to evaluate the jurisdictions of committees and generally survey the mechanics of the legislative process in the House. One possible outcome of this study is a realignment of committee jurisdictions so that most of the federal government's education support would come under one authorizing committee. You can easily see that most Hill staff persons are going to get less than a balanced and full picture of postsecondary education unless there is a disciplined effort to create the very best channels of communication possible. Sometimes this means neglecting many opportunities in order to zero in on the so-called experts and specialized sources of information. But it also means that we need to take the time to visit a campus, talk with as many professors and students as possible and, generally, to keep in touch with those persons and local programs that comprise what education is really all about. Washington can be the highest and most secluded of ivory towers.

What I have described so far is the structure and processes which are not likely to change much. Within this context we can look more specifically at past and future efforts of the postsecondary education lobby.

When I arrived on the Hill four years ago, I was advised simply to check with the American Council on Education whenever I needed input from the higher education community. Although I accepted that advice and have received invaluable assistance from ACE, it took only a few months to realize that it was an inadequate source. For one thing, ACE and the other major national associations with active federal liaison efforts represent almost exclusively the point of view of college presidents, as Mr. Quie has pointed out in the preceding chapter. It took more work to seek out thoughtful views from faculty, deans, students, trustees, state board members and staff, scholars in research centers, and others with personal experiences in the education arena. We have also begun to involve business, labor, and community service organizations.

It is imperative that Congress have access to these often divergent points of view. Although this search for differing views often frustrates the efforts of those who still believe higher education should try to present a united front to the Congress, I believe we will have a healthier, more responsive postsecondary community in the end.

Incidentally, when Mr. Quie and I use the term *postsecondary education* the use is deliberate and reflects a much different point of view than that of public policy of just a few years ago. In some respects, I believe the Congress and the Administration are considerably ahead of the campus mainstream in supporting efforts to diversify both the structure and the content of postsecondary education. As a result of this commitment, student assistance programs, for example, are now available to students in vocational/technical schools, proprietary schools, correspondence schools, and other programs besides the two- and four-year degree-granting institutions. We now think of six or seven thousand institutions in the "postsecondary" community rather than of twenty-six hundred institutions in the "higher education" community. And now we are beginning to worry about confining our attention to that education which is restricted to attendance at an institution. As more and more adults of all ages seek educational experiences to meet their unique needs and interests, traditional ways of planning and financing education must be open to question.

To get information about this diverse entity called the postsecondary community, congressmen and Hill staff are going to need better communications with a wider group of educators and others interested in education. Individuals taking the initiative and supplying us with information can provide much of what we need to learn. From my point of view, there are good ways and bad ways of doing this. The first requirement for effective lobbying is to know whom on the Hill you should reach. Chances are that there will be four or five key members or staff in both the House and the Senate who would carry the ball on any given suggestion for legislative action. For each issue the people might be different. A lobbyist needs to know the history of legislation and who has traditionally put a priority on certain kinds of federal programs. It is always good to write to or see your own congressman. Quite often he or she will then forward the idea to the appropriate committee member or staff member.

The second requirement for effective communications with the Hill is solid data. It takes less than two minutes to decide whether an office visitor did his homework. A few weeks ago I read a magazine article in which one of the Hill staff spoke about his recollections of a certain lobbyist. The pertinent section (with only the names changed) went as follows: " 'I remember when Smith first came around,' Jones recalled. 'He was emotional. He did all the talking. He made demands. He damned congressmen as do-nothing politicians. God, he came on strong. But I have a rule—that you have to distinguish between the guy who has facts and the guy who has bluster. You can tell soon enough. We see a lot of special-interest people who are mostly big talk with small arguments. The appeal of Smith was that he had a command of the facts. I was able to check them out pretty quickly and see that he was right.' "

A third factor in effective individual communications is timing. Although congressmen need to be kept constantly informed on a general basis, communications having to do with specific legislation pending before the Congress must be timely. This is one reason Washington-based lobbyists have an advantage. To a certain extent, committee work operates on a "crisis management" system—a suggestion from the outside thirty days in advance of committee action might get lost in the shuffle, while an idea submitted the day before may be too late. There is no good way to predict the best time to make a pitch, for example, on amending a specific provision of law. Reminders are often necessary. But there are days when members and staff are fishing specifically for perch and the sight of an eighteen-inch trout does little more than raise an eyebrow.

A fourth ingredient of successful lobbying is sufficient support for an idea. As you can imagine, unless it makes eminently good sense on first exposure, other people are going to have to make the same suggestion to keep it on top of the pile. And canned letters are not of much help. We believe that if a change in law is important enough, people can take the time to write a creative letter of support.

There is much more that could be said about communications with Congress. It is not a science and no one has a monopoly on it.

Higher education does communicate with Congress, but I want to persuade the postsecondary community that it can be done better and to reflect some of the complexities of the process without discouraging educators from taking individual initiative.

3

Lobbying for Limited Resources

John W. Hicks

No single approach to lobbying can be guaranteed success-ful for all time for all people. As is the case in many other human ac-tivities, however, there are certain general principles which, if applied, will increase the probability of success. I will limit my comments to lobbying at the state level, since that is where we in the public institu-tions get the bulk of our basic support, and where we can probably have the most impact either as individual institutions or as systems of institutions. In fact, current trends with respect to revenue sharing would indicate that lobbying at the state level will be even more im-portant in the future.

The most important basic principles are:

(1) Lobbying is an unglamorous, pedestrian job, that consists of day-by-day, year-by-year nurturing of attitudes held by human be-

ings with respect to higher education and the institutions which provide it.

(2) In any state, a few key leaders make the basic decision as to how much will be appropriated for higher education. The lobbyist should concentrate on developing their long-range understanding. He should not waste too much time on an obscure freshman representative who is a member of the Committees on Veterans Affairs, and Ditches and Drains. The really vital people are the governor, his fiscal staff, and a dozen key legislators. While concentrating on them, the lobbyist must be nice to everyone.

(3) In the long run, the way an institution serves is its greatest selling point. For this there is no substitute.

(4) Integrity and accountability are essential in lobbying. This is not a moral judgment, but a pragmatic one. A lobbyist caught in a lie loses his effectiveness. A public institution must be even 1000 percent accountable. There are no inappropriate questions which can be asked by a legislator about a public institution. There are stupid questions, but even these must be answered intelligently and politely.

(5) Most legislators and public officials do not have time to read long, involved treatises on higher education, nor are they easily influenced by slick gimmick publications or fancy slide shows. They do, however, need a few key facts and catchwords to orient their thinking.

(6) Faculty members are usually ineffective lobbyists, and faculty committees even less useful in lobbying than for most other purposes.

(7) Students, properly applied, can be very useful. They should be themselves, and concentrate on their own senators and representatives on a one-to-one basis when they are home on vacation or weekends. They should confine their efforts to explaining why it is important to them to have a first class education at a reasonable cost. If 10 percent of our students were to do just this, the rest of us would no longer be needed. But, of course, they never will.

(8) The purpose of a college or university is to disseminate and accumulate knowledge. No public institution should ever become involved, as an institution, in any public policy issue not directly related to higher education. Students and faculty, of course, are also citizens, and may pursue any cause they wish, but not in the name of the institution. The institution itself should remain neutral in this respect,

virtuous or popular as the cause may be. Always remember that in Hitler's Germany persecution of Jews became a "virtuous and popular" cause.

(9) The university president is a key figure in lobbying. He should develop his own style and stick to it. He should avoid overexposure, and it is useful if he can be surrounded by an aura of integrity and sincerity, and, in fact, appear a bit larger than life. He should never engage in half-truths or name-calling. Legislators would like him to wear a halo. He should try with all his might to do so.

If all of these nine points are followed, can successful lobbying be guaranteed? Of course not. So much depends on the time and the place. During the honeymoon period of the mid-1950s to the mid-1960s, almost any lobbying tactics worked, at least in the short run. If a state is broke and enrollments are declining, even the most brilliant tactician will fail. But over the long run, on a kind of market-averaging basis, these considerations are important.

Four factors are our allies in lobbying for funds for higher education. First, nearly all people are concerned about their own children's future and also about youth in general. Second, despite everything, we have tremendous faith in education in America. Third, our economy and our standard of living are still growing. And fourth, it can be demonstrated that there is a positive correlation between educational opportunity and economic development and social mobility.

These four factors also guide us in deciding what is most salable. Honest data indicating increasing enrollments almost always bring more money. This is one of the reasons for the long post World War II honeymoon for higher education, and also one of the reasons that the honeymoon is over. Data concerning inflation and unavoidable cost increases usually meet with a sympathetic hearing. People who work for a living are also aware of these cost increases and know they must be met. Increased funds to provide for academically disadvantaged students—students who previously did not go to college—are currently in favor if described properly. Programs which will increase the economic productivity of the state can often be sold and will produce additional appropriations. And currently there is interest in health-related and environmental areas.

The most difficult thing of all to sell is quality. There has always been, in public education in the United States, a strong equalitarian tendency. On balance this is probably good, but it causes difficulties for those institutions which want to consider themselves elite and to be supported by the public accordingly.

Perhaps of equal importance to the things which may be useful in selling an institution's appropriations request are the things that are counter-productive. The most important of these is criticism of a sister institution. Many times one is tempted to make invidious comparisons between one's own institution and another, to prove such things as greater efficiency, or more careful management. The aim, of course, is always to get more funds at the expense of the other school. The result, at least in the long run, is to undermine total confidence in higher education, and this probably will result in less money for all institutions.

Tearing down a sister institution usually brings retaliation, and no one is perfect enough to be without faults which can be criticized. But even if there be no retaliation, the fault pointed out in the sister institution will usually also be attributed to your own. Legislators and the public have a bad habit of generalizing about colleges and universities. This habit was especially evident during the days of campus unrest. When the media blessed us with exaggerated coverage of sit-ins on campuses several states away, many people thought all campuses were in turmoil and castigated us accordingly.

Other things probably not helpful in seeking financial support are: (1) Tearful revelations about how legislators do not understand the educational process or the sensitiveness of professors. (2) Discourses on faculty rights and prerogatives and the place of the faculty in university governance. (3) Tirades against the Federal government for its cutbacks in research support. (4) Revelations of the evils of politics, the business community, organized labor and current society in general, with the university as the last virtuous bulwark against chaos.

The vast majority (more than 90 percent) of legislators and elected public officials are honest, decent citizens, trying to do their best for the people they represent. My experience shows that state legislators represent extremely well the wishes and feelings of their constituencies. Most of them believe strongly in education and in the opportunity for young people to get an education.

Ombudsman

Francis P. Koster

The first ombudsman was appointed in Sweden in 1809. The office reflects its earlier roots in tribal custom, when a respected elder of the tribe was empowered to discuss the tribe's grievances with the chief. The modern ombudsman has held various powers, ranging from advisory to judicial. In 1954, Denmark's Parliament went so far as to empower that nation's ombudsman to prosecute errant public officials for neglect of duty. The ombudsman was directed to "Keep himself informed as to whether any person comprised by his jurisdiction pursues unlawful ends, makes arbitrary or unreasonable decisions, or otherwise commits mistakes or acts of negligence in the discharge of his or her duties."

In American higher education, the popularity of the ombudsman grew at about the same pace as the multiversity. The same era saw an increase in campus tensions, prompting the appointment of the President's Commission on Campus Unrest (also known as the Scranton Commission). This body recommended reform in campus gover-

nance, including the establishment of some kind of campus ombudsman. The need for such an official had already been perceived by some
institutions, and prior to the issuance of that Committee's report many
campuses had established the office in varying forms, beginning at
Simon Fraser Univeresity in 1965. Various other schools followed suit;
notable among them, by virtue of success (variously defined), were
Michigan State University and Cornell.

Since I worked as an ombudsman at C. W. Post Center of
Long Island University, my illustrations will be drawn from that experience. However, the dilemmas I am about to describe are common
to all colleges.

The college I worked for is tuition-dependent, private, and has
about eight thousand full-time equivalent students in its undergraduate
and graduate schools. I was responsible to, and for, all constituents,
from janitors to faculty. After two years in it, I must report that the
job of ombudsman is second in difficulty only to that of being a father.
Part of this difficulty lies in the nature of universities. Another part,
the lesser part, lies in the nature of the role of ombudsman.

The ombudsman is usually defined as a kind of inspector general. The powers of the office are: (1) the right to investigate in confidence, without restraint, either upon receipt of a complaint or on the
ombudsman's initiative; (2) the right to recommend to any official
appropriate review of the facts; (3) the right to publicize findings or
publicly criticize malfeasance. Usually, the ombudsman's office is specifically denied several powers, to wit: (1) the power to overturn any
decision of the existing authorities; (2) the power to intervene in any
situation before existing review mechanisms have been attempted. In
other words, the ombudsman is not a short cut through the power
structure. (Note, though, that the requirement is that the normal review be attempted, not exhausted. Exhaustion sets in at different times
for different people, and the complainant usually feels it long before
the bureaucracy.)

At C. W. Post Center, the office of ombudsman was established
by the president. In his public announcement to the campus community, the president said: "The ombudsman is one man you should all
be aware of, empowered to investigate on your behalf, and on behalf
of the faculty and students, any complaints, criticisms, or unfair conduct on the part of this institution. He is to be an institutional gadfly."
This mandate encompassed over eight hundred recorded complaints
in two years, dealing with everything from tenure disputes to sit-ins,

arrests, and parking tickets. I also spent a lot of time on drug cases, women's rights, and students' accusations of just about everybody of just about everything. I worked with union members, students, secretaries, and faculty committees. The office seems to have earned the respect of the campus for its effectiveness. Many of the complaints I dealt with arose from the difficulties common to all changing bureaucratic structures. Some resulted from ignorance, or represented honest mistakes. A few originated in malice. Most complaints were remedied with dispatch by the appropriate official when called to his attention. Those investigations which revealed bad administrative practice often caused the practice to be changed.

The ombudsman must employ a rhetoric that will enable the social institution to approach most closely its ideal form. This is true whether he is ombudsman in a prison, in a hospital, or in a university. When one becomes the ombudsman, he has in fact become a moral force. He symbolizes values such as fair practices and integrity. But this role inevitably carries another. The ombudsman almost inevitably becomes respected, but not liked. Worse, he must foster this righteous image if he is to do his job well. He speaks in lofty terms such as *fairness, academic freedom, due process,* and *professional ethics.* His sponsors hope that the public invocation of these terms will raise the general tenor of the institution. Judging by my experience, I believe it does.

I come now to the problem of setting the ombudsman's office in operation. When a professor grades a student unfairly, and the student seeks redress, complaining that he has been badly used and that his grade point average will drop, he is essentially complaining of a dishonest use of a system that is, itself, utterly arbitrary. Any fair-minded educator will admit that grades have little meaning in a classroom, less when compared cross-campus, and still less when used as some entity to multiply by a credit hour to achieve an average. There are other mythological structures within the academic world—for example: departments which will not recognize work done at another accredited institution as satisfying major requirements; requirements which compel students to reside in campus dormitories "for educational reasons," when the real reason is that the college has facility and construction payments to meet; universities which compel students whose legal residence is within a given radius of the school to take all their summer course work with them instead of at a more convenient, or cheaper, institution. In these last examples, the stated reason is academic, the truth is that the tuition money is needed. The phrase "students should seek the permission of the Dean" covers a multitude of such sins. Myths like these constitute a real problem for the ombudsman. The survival of his institution or of higher education as we know it today might depend on their existence. But on a pragmatic level, the existence of these practices threatens the ombudsman's effectiveness and credibility with his constituency. They, too, see the arbitrariness of such structures, and call them into question. The best I was ever able to do when confronted with such a practice was to muster a knowing wink or a helpless shrug.

Early in my tenure as ombudsman I did some serious thinking about the nature of my new power. Some research revealed that a traditional ombudsman had none, short of the glare of publicity or the threat of it. After a few mistakes, I discovered that publicity is justified only when it works, and hurts the ombudsman badly when it does not work. For example, suppose the ombudsman were to ascertain that a dubious practice, such as those I have mentioned above, was being pursued by the administration. After suitably discreet efforts at having the policy changed, he might decide that the glare of publicity was warranted. Suppose that he engenders such publicity, and the practice remains unchanged. Short of resigning, there is no further step he may take. Having tried and failed publicly, the ombudsman has exposed himself as having no power. A second or third public failure would spell the end of that ombudsman's usefulness.

Another way of looking at the same dilemma is to compare the ombudsman's power to that of a water pistol. Since it does not possess any force, it can be brandished only when one is fairly sure one need not fire it. You can attempt a holdup with a water pistol, and, if it looks real enough, it will get you by. If the need to use force becomes real, and you squirt your victim, you stand revealed. In other words, a wise ombudsman never pulls the trigger unless he is absolutely sure his victim will play dead.

There are various ways around this powerlessness, of course. One can call on someone with real power actually to implement the necessary procedure, if he will. You can also get other guys with water pistols to squirt theirs along with you. Resolutions of the faculty, straw polls of the students, commissions of inquiry, public hearings, legal advisors to the deans—they all work if aimed well. However, one must never use them unless there is certainty that they will work, or the ombudsman's colleagues in the effort will also be exposed as possessing only water guns. And that is awkward.

One neat tactic is surrender. Assess the situation, try mightily behind the scenes, invoke all sorts of allies, but if you are not going to win, do not fight and lose in public. Surrender.

An ombudsman in higher education functions within a social construct—a college or university—that is commonly held to be authentic, and it is his job to make the internal workings consistent. That the basic underpinnings do not stand close scrutiny is functionally irrelevant. In that sense, being an ombudsman is like being a father. The world is a big place, and an unjust one, and the compromises made with principle for the sake of survival are painful. Your children see you making those compromises. They may lose respect for you, or you may lose respect for yourself.

Despite the conflicts, I think the role of ombudsman is crucial to American higher education today. It is a valuable, dirty job.

PART TWO

Promoting and Marketing the Product

꘏꘏꘏꘏꘏꘏꘏꘏꘏꘏꘏꘏

As the headnote to Part One has asserted, the Watergate scandal—the Event of the Year of 1973—symbolizes two fundamental principles which, in myriad ways, are reflected back to the reader in the essays of this volume. The first of these principles, relating to political decisions, was the central subject of the essays of Part One. Part Two deals with the second fundamental principle, image-making.

According to this second principle, public confidence in a product (service, institution, or office) can be built up through the projection of the "right" image, and confidence will be maintained as long as the image remains favorable in the public eye. In the months preceding the Watergate incident, hundreds of thousands of dollars and countless man-hours of work were expended in an effort to create a favorable public image of the party in power. The stratagem might have succeeded brilliantly had its relationship to the Watergate break-in gone undetected.

The Watergate scandal has thus illustrated for the American people the power of image-building. It is the power that accounts for the prosperity of the multi-million-dollar advertising industry. But let us not simply look upon this industry disparagingly, for we must include in its definition the hundreds upon hundreds of public relations offices and lobbying groups whose task it is to project favorable images of causes and institutions that exist in the public interest and whose continued welfare we strongly support.

We should note, too, that the image-building efforts made on behalf of higher education—in recent years, at least—have not been very effective and that most members of the higher education community have not been concerned. The essays of Part One—particularly those of Quie, Andringa, and Hicks—have demonstrated how badly our image-making efforts have fared with federal and state legislatures. The essays in Part Two will show that we have done no better with respect to the business community and the general public.

These essays also point to another problem that is closely related to our public image: not only have we failed to project a favorable image, but we have also done a bad job in promoting and marketing our product among potential buyers and users. In the college and university world, the patterns of production, distribution, and consumption have gone awry. For graduate students and young holders of Ph.D.s, as the essays of Charles V. Kidd and Kenneth E. Eble (Chapters Six and Seven) vividly show, the situation has now reached all but catastrophic proportions.

The other two chapters of Part Two, however, suggest that we need not be totally pessimistic. Ernest L. Boyer's essay (Chapter Five) offers us a sound program for rebuilding public confidence in our colleges and universities. And Eugene H. Fram's essays (Chapter Eight) asks us to reject our old-fashioned attitudes and look at higher education in a new way—as a kind of business enterprise with its own peculiar marketing problems. In the new age we are about to enter, higher education will be competing with manufacturers of all sorts of other products for a piece of the nation's resources. If Fram is right, we had better learn how to package our product more attractively and market it more efficiently.

JOSEPH AXELROD

Rebuilding
Confidence

Ernest L. Boyer

Four current issues require from all educators the most careful thought and the most imaginative response: the decline in enrollments, the need for diversity, the real costs of education, and accountability.

First, the problem of depressed enrollments. There has been in the past two years a shift downward in admissions applications, and frequently we hear the charge that someone must be robbing Peter to pay Paul. It is suggested that one higher education sector is cornering too large a slice of the enrollment pie, to the detriment of competing institutions. While these charges may be true in some instances, the overall problem of enrollment decline is far more complex. It is, in fact, rooted in one of the most amazing demographic turnabouts in American history.

32

With only two exceptions, in every decade in America for the past one hundred years, this nation has had a substantial increase in its preschool (under-five-years-old) population. In more recent decades the climb was especially steep. In the 1940s, for example, the number of preschool children shot up a startling 53.4 percent. During the 1950s, the total increased by another 25 percent. The impact of this rise in the birth rate upon the nation's colleges was immense. In the heady years of the late 1950s and the early 1960s, the corridor conversations on our campuses were filled with anxious talk about the approaching avalanche of students. And there was an avalanche of sorts as the number of students in higher education rose from a little more than three million in 1960 to more than eight million in 1970.

But recently the 1970 census brought us startling news. We discovered that during the 1960s the number of preschool children had suddenly declined by three million, or 15.5 percent—a decrease twice as large as that of the depression years. And this drop took place at a time when there were more young people of childbearing age in the country than at any time in our nation's history. In other words, in a decade when America had the greatest increase of young adults in a century, it also had the sharpest decline of new babies in our entire history! With a discouraging disrespect for careful demographic projections, an entire generation of young Americans—aided by modern science—has suddenly decided to have fewer children.

So we now have in America what has been rather inelegantly labeled a "baby bust." In Massachusetts, for example, there were 116,-000 babies born in 1961, but only 89,000 blessed events were recorded in 1971. In New York State, it will mean that by 1980 the number of high school graduates will actually decline. The point is clear. The new enrollment patterns at our institutions have to do not only with how the pie is divided, but also with the declining size of the pie itself. Public and private institutions alike need to adjust to the new realities of a steady state populaton. And this challenge must be faced creatively and cooperatively. Charges of bad faith will not do, for both sectors of higher education face an entirely new enrollment situation.

A second matter of concern to both public and private institutions is the need for more diversity and flexibility in our educational programs. Even the most casual observer of the social scene can sense a special kind of ferment in our midst. Women refuse to be categorized as simply wives, housekeepers, or bunnies. Middle-aged men are returning to universities and launching new careers. Assembly line workers demand more from life than a weekly paycheck. Retirees refuse to fade wanly into the shadows. With disconcerting agility, people of all ages and all walks of life are breaking out of the neatly arranged life patterns that they were expected to follow.

But higher education, public and private alike, has all too often met this new diversity with a tortoise-like response, and still tends to cling to a fixed assortment of academic "majors" offered in a campus environment still overwhelmingly geared to the full-time residential student between the ages of seventeen and twenty-two. While one variable of the equation—the student to be served—has changed enormously, most of the other variables remain relatively intact. Lacking both far-sighted research about higher education and its constituencies and a proper flexibility, schools have too often merely imitated one another's academic styles in cookie-cutter fashion, providing the American public with a remarkably large increase in higher education but an amazingly small increase in educational choice.

In a one-product enterprise, the price of such rigidity can be high. More and more we encounter the drop-out, the step-out, the parttime student, and those who are simply bypassing the college route altogether for the world of work, travel, and self-arranged education. Not only the declining birth rates, but also consumer resistance to the flatness of the offerings, the lack of options, and the nine-to-three bankers' hours are behind the vacant space problem we are all beginning to confront.

Let me cite an example from New York State. While applications for admission have either leveled off or declined at many of New York's more traditional four-year arts and science colleges and universities (public and private), students are still being attracted to the State's specialized and community colleges, where new technical, professional, vocational, liberal arts, and continuing education courses are offered in new locations and often in new and imaginative ways, and to the State University's new non-campus Empire State College. According to the latest statistics, 1973 applications for the State University's senior colleges are down 9 percent below the corresponding point one year ago, while technical college applications have increased 5 percent, those of the specialized schools such as environmental science and forestry, maritime, agriculture, and veterinary science by 4 percent, and those of the community colleges by 3 percent.

The message, I think, is plain. Now that higher education is no longer dealing exclusively with a thin stratum of our youth, we must achieve in higher education something of the same diversity of American society itself. There is obviously a danger here of mere faddism and of compromising quality and fundamentals through a misplaced enthusiasm for relevance. But this does not negate the fact that new approaches should be tested and new programs thoughtfully introduced. Of course we have a crisis of dollars, but no less serious is the less-publicized crisis of imagination and of courage in higher education.

A third issue that should concern us all is a more prosaic, but no less vital one: the need to clarify the real costs of higher education. Beneath the smoke of the tuition battle lie some hot ashes often overlooked. For example, it is still generally assumed that today's tuition charges fail to cover more than a portion of the higher education bill. TV spot announcements as well as school catalogs repeatedly assert that tuition covers only one-third of what a college education actually costs. But the issue is not so simple. We all know that instructional costs vary significantly from level to level, increasing as the student moves up the academic ladder. The costs of educating seniors may be anywhere from 25 to 75 percent more than educating freshmen, and educating graduate and professional students may cost two, three, or, in the case of medical students, six times as much. Yet tuition charges tend to be uniform. The result is that we have reached the point where lower-level undergraduate tuition charges may actually cover *all* the instructional costs at that level, and where freshmen and sophomores are subsidizing those students in graduate and professional schools.

Such a policy may be defensible, but I feel that credibility with the public, and public understanding of higher education, would increase if we called a moratorium on sweeping generalities about education finance, and introduced more precision into fiscal analyses, distinguishing not only among various academic levels and various kinds of institutions, but also among the many different kinds of costs which make up overall budgets.

Personally, I would prefer an arrangement that linked tuition more closely to the level of instruction. As many of you may know, the State University of New York last year established an ascending scale of tuition for each level of university education: $650 lower division undergraduate, $800 upper division undergraduate, $1200 graduate, and $1600 professional degree students. We altered our tuition schedule not only because the costs rise with the educational level, but also because we think each state has a basic commitment to two years of post-secondary higher education, and because the benefits of higher education to students increase as they move further up in the programs. Of course, for a public institution, the State is still subsidizing the student at all levels, but the principle of tuition scaled to the increased costs is reflected in the scheme.

There is another college finance problem we need to face. The total bill for higher education actually includes many separate items, not all of which are equal in priority. Some costs are intimately linked to learning: faculty salaries, library costs, classroom and laboratory maintenance, and certain administrative and clerical expenses. But there also are a cluster of related programs—services that have spread across campuses during the affluent years. Some of them are housing, and food services, augmented now by health and clinical care, psychological testing, consultation, and even telephone services, parking facilities, and day care centers. It may have been acceptable to include all these auxiliary services free or at reduced rates when colleges served three or four percent of this nation's youth, as they did fifty years ago. But now that approximately 40 percent of each generation—in New York state it is 54 percent—go on to college, all universities, public and private, may need to sort out the essential from the supplemental in education, supporting the hard-core instructional costs more, and placing the others increasingly on a pay-as-you-go, full-cost, student-option basis.

Fourth, we need to face together the issue of accountability— the principle that no institution should receive funds without adequately accounting for their use to the private donors or to the taxpayers and their elected officials. (Let me make clear that I am not talking about line-by-line item presentations, but about reasonable quality control procedures.) Incredible as it seems, today's colleges and universities have yet to devise a uniform system of accounting and reporting. As a result, misleading interinstitutional comparisons are the rule, with the public hopelessly confused. We urgently need to work toward a more rational reporting system. This is especially crucial as we come to depend more and more on state and federal funds, which require precise justifications for the taxpayers. While such a proposal may seem utopian for a nation that can't even standardize its typewriter ribbons, I believe it is a must if we are to make responsible comparisons and evaluations in the field of higher learning.

Obviously such a system must never be allowed to impose a deadening uniformity. However, with a common financial language, it should be possible to establish acceptable ranges within the funding standards that would meet the imperatives of public accountability, and protect as well institutional individuality and flexibility.

As I see it then, American higher education needs to address itself to these fundamental matters if it hopes to ease the current financial squeeze. They are concerns, let me emphasize again, which transcend public-private differences—differences which have too long diverted us from matters of far greater moment.

I would like to conclude with some specific thoughts on the public support of private education. Underneath the debates about aid to higher education at both the state and federal levels there is a curious absence of solid ground. We lack the rock-hard foundation of agreed-upon principles that would guide legislation and facilitate public choice. This makes it hard for most people to distinguish between *indirect* public aid to colleges, such as scholarships for students, and *direct* aid, such as grants for institutions; between *unrestricted* grants and *mission-oriented* support; and between the kinds of aid that *states* should provide and the kinds that the *federal government* should provide. In short, we lack a policy and the principles on which to build a reasonable and enduring program of comprehensive public aid to private colleges and universities.

I would like to offer my own views on what some of these ground rules might be. In the past 20 years we have witnessed the rise of *indirect* aid to educational institutions. These programs, illustrated principally by state supported scholarship and loan programs, have promoted greater access for the poor to our colleges and have broadened the educational choices of all students by helping to narrow somewhat the public-private tuition gap. To me, indirect public aid is defensible philosophically, clear procedurally, and popular socially, and I firmly believe that such aid should not only be continued but expanded. However, the matter of *direct* aid for colleges and universities is more complicated, and understandably the debate surrounding this point is more intense. My own opinion is that direct, unrestricted aid to *any* private institution is shaky public policy as a long-term commitment. The number of private institutions in our society that could be regarded as important to the people or to their communities is huge, and public funds are necessarily limited.

What I can endorse, though, is an arrangement whereby public monies are provided to private institutions for explicitly identified public missions, under ground rules clearly understood by both the public agencies and the private institutions. What this means is that we must go beyond the loose general talk of public support for colleges because they are there, and focus instead on public needs which must be met, and which private colleges can help meet. Such mission-oriented support to private institutions by both state and federal governments has a long and highly productive record in American history. Political philanthropy also has a long record—but a far less successful or justifiable one.

Based on this principle, a wholly new pattern of public support for both public and private universities could emerge in this country. I can envision a plan in which a state identifies as precisely as possible the special educational tasks it wishes to see undertaken and sets the accountability standards that must be met. In such a circumstance, not just the state colleges and universities but all the institutions of higher education in the state would be viewed as a single resource that could help carry out selected educational tasks. The publicly supported institutions would, of course, continue as the chief vehicle for meeting the higher education needs of the public, but private colleges and universities in those states where private resources are available might wish to affiliate with the public institutions to meet specific, high priority obligations. Thus, the board of trustees of each private college in the state might study those public educational tasks where additional help is needed, weigh the pros and cons of joining the effort to meet them, and vote the institution in or out of the program of state aid. This procedure would not only meet the test of responsibility in public policy and public spending, but would also maintain the dignity and independence of the private colleges in the partnership. It would allow certain private colleges to receive, without jeopardizing their private status, public funds in return for a commitment to share in carrying out specific educational tasks. And it would reduce the fears of public universities that unrestricted state funding of private institutions would drain the public treasury, while still leaving the job of meeting the growing number of public educational tasks to the public colleges.

What I envision, then, is a new kind of institutional relationship in our midst—a kind of third force in higher education. This development would not be entirely novel. A few states have already moved in this direction, although most have not clearly defined the public missions or the accountability procedures. And several of the nation's most eminent universities in effect have moved toward a "federal-affiliated" status through their enormous commitments to carrying out national missions and research.

Let me offer two brief illustrations of what I have in mind. Since nearly every state is under pressure to provide opportunities for two years of postsecondary education—the 13th and 14th years of education are now viewed almost as a right, like high school education— and since our complicated world *does* demand more highly educated persons, states might come to view *all* the higher education facilities in their state as a potential resource to meet their education demands, not just the public colleges. Such an approach would seem justified, because this is the level at which the enrollment crunch at the public colleges is most intense. Every private college willing to share more fully in the education of people at these lower undergraduate levels— perhaps even by establishing within their college a special "mini-college"—could receive a direct, per-student subsidy for every freshman and sophomore state resident they enroll. Another illustration relates to the problem of upper-division college programs. In many states we have a growing transfer problem as students, particularly from our community colleges, press for upper-division work in fields now in short supply. But several of the private colleges and universities have undersubscribed upper-division programs in these fields. In such circumstances, a state institution might have an affiliate relationship with these private institutions for selected services rather than duplicate the same programs in the next county. Good public policy suggests that public aid be directed not simply to meet self-defined survival needs, but rather to achieve the more rational and defensible goal of using college resources collectively to help meet what most taxpayers agree are important public needs.

As for federal aid to higher education, it seems to me that the same procedure could apply—the linking of aid to colleges and universities with public service, in this case with national policy concerns. Three that come to mind are these: (1) the promotion of equality of access, as illustrated by the Basic Opportunity Grants; (2) second, the support of key professional needs which transcend the interest of any single state, leading to support for professional schools of medicine and public health, for example; (3) third, the stimulation of research in areas of high priority, such as ending pollution, improving the cities, or finding the origins of cancer, and in those fields which help maintain a strong international posture. At both the state and federal levels,

it all adds up to the conclusion that public resources should be shared
to the extent that clearly defined public obligations are shared.

To conclude with the observation with which I began, the issue
is not simply money. The issue is this: What are we, together, willing
to do to clarify issues, rebuild our structures, and recapture the zest
and momentum which once characterized our effort? The task will
not be easy. As John Gardner put it a decade ago: "We like to think
that institutions are shaped according to the best men in them, and
sometimes they are . . . But that is not the only way institutions get
shaped. Sometimes institutions are the sum of the historical accidents
that have happened to them. Like the sand dunes in the desert, they
are shaped by influence but not by purposes." But Dr. Gardner went
on to express the conviction—and it is a conviction which I share—
that "men can shape their institutions to suit their purposes—provided
they are clear as to what those purposes are; and provided they are
not too gravely afflicted with the diseases of which institutions die—
among them complacency, myopia, [and] an unwillingness to choose."[1]

[1] John Gardner, "The Future of the University," address given at the
inauguration of President James Perkins, Cornell University, October 4, 1963.

6

Doctorate Output: Overproduction or Underconsumption?

Charles V. Kidd

Whether we are over-producing or under-using doctorates for both current and future use is one of the central points of philosophy and theory facing graduate education. The question is not only theoretical; it is practical in the highest degree because it affects such matters as federal appropriations, state decisions on the establishment and dismantling of doctoral programs, and the career choices of individuals.

What does the future hold?

One approach to estimating what the future holds might be

called the conventional supply-demand analysis, that is, a series of assumptions that yield estimates of the number of doctorates to be awarded in the future and the number who will be absorbed in different lines of work. The National Science Foundation, for example, has used these assumptions for the demand side: (1) an increase in graduate/undergraduate faculty in proportion to projected growth of enrollments, with the Ph.D. share of faculty rising at "judgmental" rates; (2) future employment of Ph.D.s at some academic research and development (R&D) jobs equal to the ratio of expected R&D, taken as a constant share of GNP, to the cost of R&D per worker, based on a weighted trend projection of the growth of costs; (3) a growth of non-academic, non-R&D jobs at 1960–1968 rates of change; (4) estimated "growth" of demand for new Ph.D.s due to death or retirement based on historic death and working life tables.

On the supply side, the NSF projections focused largely on the number of new science-engineering Ph.D.s, determined by applying various ratios to the estimated number of future baccalaureates, taken from Office of Education extrapolations based on demographic developments. The number of bachelor's degrees is multiplied by trend-projected ratios of (1) science baccalaureates to all bachelor's degrees, (2) first-year graduate science enrollments to bachelor of science degrees, (3) total science graduates to first-year enrollments, (4) doctorates awarded to total enrollments three years earlier to obtain estimates of numbers of Ph.D. graduates. The estimates are then adjusted for immigration and emigration on the basis of historic experience to yield a net supply projection. While the NSF projection dealt with scientists and engineers in particular, their technique can be applied to all fields.

To what conclusions do these forecasts lead? Allan Cartter, who first pointed out that we should be worried about oversupply rather than shortages in 1980, notes that the time of trouble has arrived sooner than he had originally predicted. Most forecasts are now less optimistic than they have been in earlier years. For example, the NSF said of its 1971 projections that they represent a greater likelihood of a future oversupply than the projections developed two years earlier. In 1973, therefore, the possibility of oversupply should be viewed as a matter of continuing concern, and not as a passing aberration.

However, it appears from the NSF forecasts that there will be a rough balance between demand and supply for scientists and engineers, with some probable imbalance in specific fields. There may be substantially more engineering Ph.D.s than will find suitable work, although virtually all of them will have jobs. This may also be the case in mathematics and the social sciences, but the imbalance may not be as severe as in the case of engineering. The outlook is for reasonable balance in the physical sciences.

If there is not to be substantial unemployment among scientists and engineers, many more than the current 10 percent—as many as 15 or 20 percent—will have to be employed in nonacademic, non-research and development employment. This includes such fields as management, sales, government administration, consultation, and teaching in junior colleges and high schools. Here one faces the question whether such employment proves that there has been "overproduction." I think not, for the reason that these are worthy and productive careers. Moreover, a consistent line of development in this country, and one which has contributed greatly to social mobility and economic growth, has been a steady elevation of the level of education of those in given lines of work. However, this line of argument cannot be pushed too far, because at an extreme it offers a way of dismissing any level of overproduction. That is, those not absorbed in academic work in four-year colleges and universities and in nonacademic research and development are simply assumed to be productively employed in other categories.

According to the supply-and-demand projections, there may well be many more doctors of education than can be absorbed, and it appears that there will be many more holders of doctorates who want academic jobs of all kinds than there will be jobs for them to fill.

Now, what criticisms can be made of these supply-demand forecasts? One problem is that forecasts in the social sciences are not simply efforts to foretell what will happen. They can and often do influence the course of events. For example, a forecast of overproduction of engineers with Ph.D.s can be one of the factors which leads to a decrease in enrollment and eventually in the output of Ph.D.s. If the forecasts are in error, harm may be done.

The problem is further complicated by the long time required to produce a Ph.D. and by the long working life of the average Ph.D. A student who is pondering whether to become a Ph.D. candidate must, so far as job prospects influence him, consider not the current market but the market when he first looks for a job five years later and the market over the succeeding thirty years of his working life. To the extent that people believe manpower forecasts and act upon them, the forecasts are doomed to error unless those who make them predict the effects of their own forecasts. The more widely the forecasts are publicized the greater the extent to which they become an active factor influencing the trend of events.

Another problem associated with some forecasts is a tendency to use highly refined occupational categories. Sometimes unrealistic efforts are made to match holders of specific, specialized degrees against estimated jobs in these same specialized fields. This over-specificity ignores two important facts. First, people can and do change their specific fields of endeavor. Second, jobs themselves change. Obviously, the further into the future one looks, the broader the aggregates of occupations should be.

A more fundamental criticism relates to the methods of forecasting. The key deficiency is the failure to take into account the effect of a changed relationship between supply and demand on salaries, on the willingness and ability of various kinds of employers to hire doctorates when salary levels change, and on individuals' decisions to undertake graduate work. After all, the operation of the market does exert self-correcting forces. If there are more Ph.D.s than there are jobs, salaries for them will tend to go down (or increase less rapidly) relative to other salaries, and fewer people will take doctorate training. One may argue about how effectively these market forces operate, but their existence cannot be denied, nor their tendency to restore balance in the market.

All in all, I am persuaded that forecasts which ignore these market forces—and this includes virtually all of them—seriously overstate the future output of doctorates and understate the demand for them. For example, the leveling off of graduate enrollment in the fall of '71 and '72 was not anticipated by the forecasters. A serious effort to quantify the market forces is urgently needed, because some bad policy mistakes are being made on the basis of bad forecasts. Serious as this methodological flaw is, those who emphasize it basically accept the utility of forecasting on a supply-demand basis and undertake to improve the process.

However, there are two other approaches which reject the forecasting approach root and branch. The first of these contends that one should concentrate not on prospective demand as measured by cold economic analysis, but upon the needs of society. This basic idea has been developed most fully by Ted Vaughan and Gideon Sjoberg,[1] who criticize all forecasts based on estimates of demand. Their argument questions how one can speak seriously of over-production of highly trained people when there are obviously tremendous unmet needs in many sectors of society. The conventional measure of demand for academic jobs ignores the development of patterns of lifetime learning. The continuing growth of the service sector means that ever-larger segments of the work force will need advanced training. The knowledge explosion will require retraining of professions on a vast scale. A serious attack on environmental problems will generate large-scale needs for people with advanced training. As the work week decreases and the average retirement age is lowered, there will be a need to use education to improve the quality of life.

As a separate line of argument, Vaughan and Sjoberg say that supply-demand analyses of the usual kind, and specifically Allan Cartter's analyses, are consciously or unconsciously political instruments. A quotation will indicate the line of argument.

It is unfortunate that Cartter has chosen to accept the traditional image of education as immutable. His assumptions concerning the ideal proportion of Ph.D.s in colleges and an ideal student-teacher ratio of 20 to 1 means that educators are locked into a structure that may not be sufficiently flexible to cope with drastically changing social conditions. . . . Certainly, alternatives must be explored if higher education is to deal effectively with the issue of quality of life instead of emphasizing the training of persons to match specific occupations within the society.

In sum, Cartter's thesis of the overproduction of Ph.D.s and his proposed response to this condition shift attention from the basic issues and problems in graduate education, which demand a reordering of national priorities, to issues that are solvable within the present political framework. Our thesis is that the problem Cartter has defined is one of political allocation of resources and is not one of too many people with too much education. It is a condition that leaders of higher education should aggressively counter. It is not a condition that we should rush to justify intellectually. . . . Cartter's analysis shifts attention from the important task evaluating and restructuring doctoral programs to that of accepting and legitimatizing the constraints placed upon graduate education.[2]

[1] "The Politics of Projection: A Critique of Cartter's Analysis," *Science,* Vol. 177, No. 4044 (July 14, 1972), pp. 142–147.

[2] Vaughan and Sjoberg, "The Politics of Projection," p. 146.

I separate two lines of thought in this approach to assessing the future. First, all of the elements of the argument relating to possible sources of jobs clearly ought to be taken into account. For example, if a failure to assess the effects of such developments as open admissions on the number of academic jobs has resulted in an understatement of demand for people with advanced degrees, this should be corrected. This applies to all of the points made by those who take the "needs" approach. However, it would be a serious mistake to equate in importance aspirations for a better world, or a desire to see deficiencies in the society and the economy done away with, or impatience with the rate of change in social and political institutions with the availability of jobs in the future. Vaughan and Sjoberg make this mistake, and it leads to many indefensible assertions and unsound arguments.

It is true that many assumptions relating to demand and supply rest on judgments as to what the political process will produce in the way of governmental programs and appropriations. As one example, the assumption that the student-faculty ratio will remain at 20:1 implies a judgment that funds for education will not increase at a rate which could make a lower ratio possible. An assumption of a 4 percent long-run annual increase in GNP represents a judgment that the entire set of forces generating GNP will not operate so as to produce a higher rate. Clearly, these judgments should be explicit when forecasts are made, and for the most part they have been.

Vaughan and Sjoberg go further and claim that forecasters, such as Cartter, are actually advocates of the assumptions made for the forecasts. This is nonsense. One can legitimately point out large and important unmet needs in society as part of a political effort to move things in a direction that is philosophically congenial. Perhaps those who have made forecasts should be more active politically, and if they want to avoid being scolded by Vaughan and Sjoberg they had better be pretty liberal. But this process should be kept entirely separate from efforts to project what will actually happen in the fuure.

A more sophisticated and telling set of objections to conventional demand-supply analysis has been raised by Howard Bowen,[3] who claims that the character of the economy cannot be predicted for periods long enough to be pertinent to educational planning—that is thirty to sixty years in the future. Manpower requirements depend on

[3] "Manpower Management and Higher Education," *Educational Record,* Vol. 54, No. 1 (Winter 1973), pp. 5–14.

what the country wants to do, and education itself is an active force affecting the future. There need be no fear of "oversupply" based upon estimates of future supply and demand because the economy will adapt to various levels of supply. Education, and even training, that is not used for the expected purpose is not wasted. "A Ph.D. in English or history may find his destiny in journalism, in the State Department, in publishing, or in secondary education." Therefore (and this is my extrapolation from Bowen's premise) we need not be worried about the unemployment of those with a doctorate.

Bowen concludes: "Education at all levels is not something to be feared but something to be encouraged. It should not be 'strait jacketed' by detailed central planning based on labor market considerations. Central planning of the educational system, which implies rationing places in various programs, is not only unnecessary but almost certainly harmful. . . . The number of places in various programs and in the whole system would be set in response to student choices, not in response to dubious labor market projections."[4]

Finally, he makes the point that the manpower theory of educational planning "is based on a grand misconception—the input-output or the means-ends fallacy—that permeates society. The world is regarded as divided into inputs, primarily in the form of work or effort, and outputs, primarily in the form of economic goods and services." He points out that inputs can be rewarding and exhilarating, and that outputs can be stultifying. "Education is not designed to prepare people for whatever work flows from the blind and predestined imperative of technology; rather it is intended to educate people of vision and sensitivity, who will be motivated to direct technology into humanly constructive channels."[5] I find this philosophy congenial, a wise guide to public policy, and one diametrically opposed to the current philosophy of the Nixon Administration with respect to the support of doctoral training.

However, despite my agreement with Bowen's major premises, I have some reservations about his analysis. The first is that an effort to project is not necessarily an effort to establish central planning. Good projections can and should make personal choice better informed. The second reservation is that federal expenditures for graduate education and for support of graduate students are based to a large degree upon presumed shortages in the future in specific occu-

---

[4] "Manpower Management," p. 11.
[5] "Manpower Management," p. 14.

pational areas. This does call for a certain degree of central planning. Indeed, any federal support for graduate education and for graduate students calls for a certain kind and degree of central planning. This is the case because the money must be made available for a purpose, or a set of purposes, and the amount of money made available ought to be determined by the net utility (measured on the basis of some criteria) of expenditures for graduate education as compared with the utility of expenditure on other things. Actually, I believe that the future supply-demand situation should be one factor in guiding federal action, but that it should not be as important as it is now. And above all, the stress upon the *current* state of the labor market makes no sense.

In my judgment, the rationalization of the federal role based upon manpower supply and demand is narrow and inadequate, but it is the philosophy which prevails. In this circumstance, it seems to me that the wisest course of action is to work hard to make forecasts more sophisticated and realistic, rather than to give up because they have been poor in the past or because they may be misused.

☙ 7 ☙

Graduate Students and the Job Market

Kenneth E. Eble

Among recent speculations about the future of higher education, the most pessimistic is Lyman Glenny's speech to the 1973 annual meeting of the Association of American Colleges.[1] Glenny predicts that the great age of expansion in college enrollments is over, and that the proportion of state and federal budgets going to higher education has reached a plateau. These harsh realities, Mr. Glenny observes, are likely to be more readily acknowledged by those outside of higher education than by faculty and administrators within. In regard to the faculty, I can corroborate Glenny's claim by quoting from a recent item in the *Salt Lake Tribune*. Addressing a group of high school seniors, Robert Parry, a professor of chemistry, stated: "There

[1] "Emerging State Systems of Higher Education and Institutional Autonomy," speech to Association of American Colleges, Jan. 15, 1973.

is always room in the most crowded disciplines for an enthusiastic, able
and hard-working person. . . . I believe it is clear that predictions
in manpower needs haven't really been very good. One might even
say they are dead wrong. They certainly could provide no sound basis
for selecting a career."[2] I find it grimly ironic that in the same section of the paper another item read, "Population Predictions Revised
Downward Again." I have recently been told by faculty members at
various schools that the hundreds of letters graduate students write to
get no jobs are misleading; that the hundreds of letters department
chairmen get applying for positions they don't have are deceiving; and
that the junior colleges still comprise a good job market for holders of
M.A. and Ph.D. degrees. All these contentions are, I think, dead
wrong.

There are, it should be said, some speculations on the optimistic side. Two Columbia University sociologists, Abram Jaffee and
Walter Adams, predict a "massive escalation" in the demand for graduate and professional education during the next two decades.[3] *The
Chronicle of Higher Education,* from which I took this note, reports
that graduate school enrollments were up by about 2 percent this fall
and that applications for 1973 appeared to be increasing as well.[4]

Two more predictions follow (from sources which should be
very knowledgeable about graduate education) the first of which has
already proved to be strikingly wrong: In *The Knowledge Revolution,*
a book published in 1968, Gustave Arlt, then president of the Council
of Graduate Schools, said, "Obviously the demand for highly trained
brain power for business, industry, education, and government will
continue to rise. Just as obviously America will not produce it in sufficient numbers."[5] Arlt was at the time worried about the Selective
Service Act—"this insane piece of legislation"—which he said threatened to reduce the number of Ph.D.s from a projected 24,900 in 1971
to 14,940. The actual number of degrees conferred in 1968–1969 was
26,100, and in 1972 32,000. In a 1970 study, Lewis Mayhew concludes that if institutional ambitions are fulfilled, sixty to seventy thousand Ph.D.s may be conferred in 1980. "In spite of conflicting evi-

---

[2] *Salt Lake Tribune,* Mar. 2, 1973.
[3] "Graduate-School Applications Rise, Reversing Trend of Recent
Years," *The Chronicle of Higher Education,* Mar. 5, 1973.
[4] *Ibid.*
[5] D. N. Chorafas, *The Knowledge Revolution* (New York: McGraw-
Hill, 1968), preface.

dence," Mayhew writes, "institutional leaders tend to believe that shortages of faculty will persist in all save a few fields well into the 1970s and probably beyond."[6]

Let me comment briefly about these predictions. My own pessimism as to future prospects for an abundance of suitable jobs for M.A. and Ph.D. degree holders rests upon four related facts. The first is the basic population patterns which have already reduced public school enrollments almost everywhere. The approach to zero population growth has been upon us since the mid-60s. Though population patterns could change, the changes which will affect college enrollments in the eighties have already taken place. The second fact is that the proportion of young people going on to college has steadily increased throughout the century. From around 4 percent in 1900, it has today passed 50 percent in some states, and is between 35 to 40 percent nationally. While there is still a large pool of prospective college students in the general population, that pool is strikingly smaller than it has been in the past. A third related fact is that increasing the size of the college-going population significantly is dependent upon increasing financial support for higher education. Although, theoretically, the country could afford a continuing expansion of graduate work, the pattern of spending in the past does not justify much optimism. The increase in the percentage of the GNP going to higher education—up to 2 percent in the 1960s—seems to have leveled off. State budgets provide 30 percent of the direct costs of graduate study, and increases from this source seem to be closely tied to increased enrollments. Certainly, the ratio of faculty to students could go up, thus increasing the need for faculty. In the recent period of slowed growth and financial exigency, however, that ratio for many hard-pressed schools has gone down. And, certainly, the pressure from an ever-growing number of unemployed Ph.D.s could expand the job market. It could also hold salaries down, decrease fringe benefits, and in other ways put strong pressures upon decreasing the supply. The final fact is that the expanding job market for M.A.s and Ph.D.s was largely created by the colleges and universities themselves. Dr. Arlt is not being very precise when he talks about the demand for advanced brain power from business, industry, education, and government. For what the facts said then, and what they say now, is that higher education is the major employer of the products of its graduate schools. Though

[6] L. B. Mayhew, *Graduate and Professional Education, 1980* (New York: McGraw-Hill, 1970), p. 20.

there are exceptions in some fields, and there might be more exceptions if the nature of graduate study would substantially change, in a majority of fields the majority of Ph.D. recipients find employment in higher education. In biology in the period 1963–1967, for example, 70 percent of the Ph.D.s became college teachers. In English, a major producer of Ph.D.s in the humanities, the percentage has always run higher.

My point is not to argue the absolute or even relative rightness of pessimistic predictions about graduate education. It is rather that everyone involved in graduate study should begin to take seriously the implications of greatly changed conditions of employment and support in the decades ahead. The beginning recognition is that most graduate students, particularly Ph.D.s, become teachers, and at institutions at some remove from the graduate schools from which they took their degrees. Without a great increase in undergraduate enrollments, the demand for new college teachers will drop sharply. According to the Newman report, even during the expansion of the 1960s, only 25 percent of the demand for faculty was as replacements for faculty members who retired or died. Using very low figures (45,000) for doctorates produced in 1980, only one in four will be needed for college teaching.

Against these discouraging prospects, what can one say that graduate students might want to know about the teaching business, except beware? First, if graduate students persist in the face of the odds, and I hope some will, they should expect to take teaching more seriously than it has been taken in the past. I am not sure they will get much help from the profession or from the institutions in which they find jobs. Nevertheless, hard times have a way of emphasizing that the teaching market is the main market for Ph.D.s. Though there is a chance that publication will become even more of a forced growth than now in the face of increased competition to get and hold jobs, there are some other forces working in the opposite direction. In most of the traditional liberal arts subjects, enrollments are down. Undergraduate students, freed from a required curriculum, are not conforming to the patterns that specialized research interests have laid upon departments. Majors no longer see the graduate school as an automatic path to a career, or even as an alternative to what is next best. With the need to hold students, to court students even, the teacher who can hold and attract students may have the edge. Even now, teachers who have special skills in dealing with the more diversified student body characteristic of undergraduate education are probably more employable than those prepared for traditional spots. If Ph.D. students expand their concept of teaching, jobs may open up in those enterprises—like Britain's Open University—which prepare materials for new contexts of teaching and learning or serve in other ways in those new educational settings.

Second, instead of running scared and toeing the old departmental lines, graduate students might push the faculty to broaden the employment opportunities for graduate students. Faculty members are not impervious to their students' collective plight. If graduate students keep the application letters coming, but large numbers of new teaching jobs do not materialize, the pressure for alternatives to college and university teaching careers will rise. In my own discipline—English— I can think of a greatly expanded effort to produce information specialists, experts in the use of language who might give the universities themselves badly-needed help in handling the flow of information. The Newman report calls for a shift from primary emphasis on "internally oriented" graduate programs to "externally oriented" ones. In most disciplines, some of the intelligence and energy which now goes into advancing a very academic kind of knowledge, might be better focused upon expanding the opportunities for gainful employment, both for the individual and the society.

Third, my advice to graduate students is do not opt for a career as a college or university professor unless you have an aptitude for teaching, and do not take your own word for that. Do not think of it as something that can be done on the side, or that it is easy. Do not regard it as elevating you above those who earn an honest living. Above all, resist the divine afflatus toward advanced study which the graduate schools have been very successful in establishing in too many of their graduates. I quote from a letter I received when I was directing the Project to Improve College Teaching. It was written by an associate professor (of English, I shamefully admit), who was disturbed over the project's emphasis upon the importance of teaching in the preparation of graduate students. My correspondent wrote: "The modern Ph.D. is one of the most rigorous and demanding intellectual exercises to which the human mind is subjected. Its satisfactory completion requires not only a mind of considerably better than average powers of concentration, discrimination, analysis, and synthesis, but a large amount of time devoted to intense mental effort and the accumulation of an immense store of facts and theories requiring long study and memorization. . . . One who is already expending this amount of time and effort in a field which is necessarily the center of his interest cannot reasonably be required to achieve some level of skilled performance in a second field, *entirely unrelated* to his interest, before he is allowed to practice in his chosen area. This is a requirement imposed on no other profession, and which no other profession would tolerate." That second, "entirely unrelated" field, in case the reader missed it amidst the exaltation, is college teaching.

Fourth, it seems to me that the most pressing task of graduate study is that of examining the attitudes the universities have toward knowledge itself. I believe we are at a point in history where we need to arrive at new understanding of and new attitudes toward knowledge. Bacon's position in the seventeenth century provides an example of another such time, but the Baconian advancement of learning may be as much the target for a modern Bacon as scholasticism was Bacon's target. Graduate students in literature, philosophy, history—in science for that matter—should seize upon the challenge such an inquiry offers.

In lesser but related ways, graduate students could assist in re-evaluating much that goes on in the graduate school. The day the phrase "genuine contributions to knowledge" disappears from the graduate catalogues will be an auspicious day for learning. A number of other terms could also go. *Research,* for example, as the single constricting term for a great many praiseworthy activities which should not have to be sneaked into advanced study. *Research* surely should be a lower-case word, an honorable sub-activity highly favored in some disciplines, inappropriate in others. *Production,* particularly when we are threatened by over-production, should be replaced by a less factory-oriented term. And since we are worried about how many of whatever it is that graduate schools produce society will support, we might examine just what we mean by *master, doctor,* and *philosophy.*

Finally, since none of the above suggestions are likely to be carried out easily, graduate students should learn to resist much of what goes on in graduate study. There are those, mainly in the physical sciences, who express a reasonably high degree of satisfaction with graduate work. In the humanities, satisfaction is less pronounced. But over the years, the harsh denunciations of graduate study have been remarkably similar and have come from many different quarters. One of the latest of these comes from Stanford's "Study of Graduate Education." In a minority report submitted by Mark Mancall, associate professor of history, this dismal picture of the Ph.D. student is set forth: "Having worked toward the degree by taking a requisite number of units, fulfilling special requirements, achieving a certain grade average, passing qualifying examinations, and writing an often crushingly boring dissertation, the graduate student, his imagination probably restricted and dulled, his mind perhaps withered and exhausted, his soul jaded, his enthusiasm gone, is transformed by the magic of a degree into an educator charged with the responsibility of imparting to those who come after him the excitement of learning and a sense of the high adventure in ideas."[7] The language is overblown, perhaps, but is not much different than that William James used to describe the Ph.D. Octopus in 1903. The cast of characters has hardly changed at all.

[7] H. Packer (ed.), *Graduate Education* (Stanford, California: Stanford University), p. 71 (Volume VII of *The Study of Education at Stanford*).

8

Marketing Higher Education

Eugene H. Fram

Problems faced by higher education in the last several years have led some educators to conclude that a business-minded approach to education has merit. In other words, institutions of higher learning may look toward business for help in finding solutions to some of their problems. Terms such as cost-benefit analysis, management by objectives, and systems analysis are now included in the language of college and university administrators. It is becoming clear that problems faced by business organizations are not much different from those faced by any human organization, although organizational outputs may be different.

Business approaches in use by colleges and universities have largely been drawn from the financial practices of the business community, but another business function—marketing—has recently been identified as an area in which a business approach might benefit higher education. In fact, marketing principles may be of greater value than financial principles in solving educational problems. In the business sector, the job of the marketing function is to help the organization focus on the needs and wants of current and potential customers. If marketing approaches are applied to institutions of higher learning, they can similarly help the college or university focus on its "customers" —students, alumni, donors, and governmental agencies. For example, one writer has concluded that a faculty member is really trying to *sell* an idea when he submits a research proposal.[1]

The aim of this paper is to take pragmatic steps (1) to show that the decision variables and histories of both fields are similar; (2) to describe the marketing philosophy which some businesses have used to solve their problems and to maintain growth; and (3) to provide guidelines which educators can use to benefit from the business experience.

Those who make decisions in business and education are confronted with controllable and uncontrollable variables.[2] Uncontrollable variables, obviously, are those which the person making a decision must assess but which he can not directly control—such things as culture, the general economic environment, and social trends. These affect the future and the well-being of both the educational institution and the business organization.

On the other hand, there are four variables clearly within the decision-making power of those in higher education and in the commercial world: (1) The curriculum or service of an educational institution corresponds to the product or service of a business. What shall it be and to whom should it be offered? (2) The location of services— on-campus, off-campus, for example, or by TV—corresponds to business decisions about distribution of goods, and the movement and storage of them. (3) Communication with students, prospective students, alumni, donors, and the general community may be likened to promotional practices in business. (4) Tuition levels which will enable schools to serve the greatest number of students in a financially efficient manner may be compared to prices.

Institutions of higher education and business organizations have

---

[1] A. R. Krachenberg, "Bringing the Concept of Marketing to Higher Education," *Journal of Higher Education*, July 1972, p. 370.

[2] For further discussion of this model in business, see E. J. McCarthy, *Basic Marketing: A Managerial Approach* (Homewood, Ill.: Irwin, 1971).

faced similar problems in the past because of a failure to respond to customer demand. Glenny reports that from the 1830s to the 1850s college enrollment dropped because the Latin and Greek classical education provided did not seem relevant to the times.[3] As a result, land grant agricultural and mechanical arts colleges were developed. In a similar fashion, traditional retailers were slow to respond to changes in marketing needs after World War II, and the discount store approach took hold and has continued to flourish. On the other hand, the concept of Xerography was very difficult to market initially. In essence, history has indicated that both the institution of higher learning and the business organization can suffer by being unresponsive to current needs, and great effort may be required to achieve success with a new concept.

In the 1950s, business competition began to heighten as wartime production capacity was redirected to the manufacture of civilian goods. The marketing community developed a philosophy or approach that is commonly called the *marketing concept,* which calls upon business to gear itself first to assessing customer needs and wants and then to manufacturing goods (or providing services) to meet these needs and wants. (In contrast, *product philosophy* begins with a manufactured product thought to have a good chance of sales success, and then the sales department is given the responsibility for planning and implementing the necessary promotional effort. The product may be successful, if it *happens* to meet a need.) The *marketing concept* demands that company policies be built on a base of customer needs and wants, while the *product concept* focuses on sale of a given product. Although the difference may seem semantic, the operational consequences can be substantial. The difference is that the marketing concept calls for serious "research" of the market prior to introduction, while the product concept calls for continual attempted selling of developed products, some of which may not have a market. Historically the 1830–1850 situation discussed by Glenny provides a good example of this in higher education. Colleges and universities were attempting to sell classical education, while the market wanted a more applied curriculum. Are many schools today using a product approach when in reality they should be using a marketing approach?

Kotler and Dubois summarize the situation with the following

[3] L. A. Glenny, "The Changing Milieu of Postsecondary Education—a Challenge to Planners," keynote address delivered to the National Higher Education Management Seminar, Oct. 16, 1972.

analysis: "Rather than adjust to current student desires, they [one class of universities] prefer to sell it [education] as a product that consumers should want. They resort to a classic persuasion strategy, which is to change the consumers' attitudes rather than the product. . . . The other class of universities have, along with the students, some misgivings about their product and above all see the necessity of it being seen as desirable in terms of the 'purchaser's' standards. So they venture to find what students and the society-at-large want, and then attempt to reshape their product into one that meets market desires."[4]

General Electric, in the industrial world, is credited with being the first company to formally adopt a marketing viewpoint (in 1952) as corporate policy, and the electric can opener and electric knife are successful products which were developed from its utilization. Today it would be difficult to find a business organization which would not openly subscribe to the viewpoint, but putting the state of mind into operation is hard. Many firms in reality still work on a product philosophy, and as a result the rate of new product failure remains high.

Most of the problems businessmen have experienced in implementing the marketing concept center around getting the basic marketing assessments. In all types of profit and nonprofit, human-oriented activities, projection of the future environment is difficult. It comes down to the old problem that there is often a difference between what customers say they will do and what they actually do. In fact, customers often are not aware of their own needs and wants, and to listen to "surface" statement can lead to disaster. These difficulties are often paralleled in higher education. One college, as an example, made a serious error when they accepted student statements as guidelines for dormitory room size. The students indicated, on the surface, they wanted large lounge areas at the expense of room size. After the building was completed it was discovered the lounges weren't used very much, and the small rooms were causing many morale problems. A marketing approach to this question would have called for a more sophisticated analysis of student living styles.

Compounding assessment difficulties are the uncontrollable variables, such as the economic climate. The recent economic recession has changed many views on what a higher education can and should do for a student. Despite all the difficulties described above, a substan-

---

[4] P. Kotler and B. Dubois, "A Marketing Orientation for Colleges and Universities," working paper, Northwestern University, July 1972, p. 12.

tial number of business organizations have successfully utilized the marketing approach and have continually attempted to probe the market in order to better serve their customers. The marketing man does this with the realization that "nothing happens until a sale is made." And sales depend upon customers perceiving value in what is being sold. Similarly, the institution for higher education must offer something of value to students, donors and others in order to survive. For example, auxiliary services beyond education may be important to students. Some schools have recently established day care centers (as a service device) so that mothers can attend classes. This has been a radical departure for schools.

Although difficult, the assessment problem encountered by the marketing fraternity has been amenable to partial solution through various types of research plus some "simple-minded fact-finding." Marketing men have borrowed heavily from the academic disciplines; and consequently the academic community, in its turn, has a wealth of approaches to utilize in solving its assessment problems with familiar tools. In business, the marketing approach has had impact on both people and processes. Its widespread use in academia should have a similar effect.

The faculty, as do salesmen in a business organization, have continual contact with an important group of customers, the students. If they are to function effectively, they must come to the understanding that they are salesmen for the institution. This does not mean either that they should be hired or fired by students, as in the medieval university, or even that the customers are always right. In fact, experience has shown that they often do not understand their own needs and wants. The faculty member has an obligation in undergraduate education to help the student mature, which means that he must hold standards at least equal to those of the outside world which the student will face upon graduation. This is not always easy in many fields where "real world" standards are ambiguous.

On the other hand, selling the student means that the professor is easily accessible for guidance, has empathy for student problems and concerns, and interacts with the student on some meaningful basis. This type of relationship is quite opposite to the sterile environment where the professor provides a series of lectures plus two or three examinations.

As a salesman, the professor must help his customers to use a product.[5] Simple observation of the marketing process shows the concern of many producers with helping the customer obtain maximum benefit from product utilization. Instructions are given as completely as possible, and, with certain more costly items, a good sales approach requires post-purchase contact of some sort. This activity has been subject to much study, because the facts show that satisfied customers tend to transmit their satisfaction to other buyers.

Many professors are so concerned with the subject matter they are teaching that they pay only very little attention to the use students make of their education. Some may even encourage students to prepare for fields which are currently overcrowded and will continue to be overcrowded for a number of years in the future. For example, some universities continue to expand Ph.D. programs despite obvious problems in the academic marketplace.

Professors, in particular, and the academic community in general, have the responsibility to provide a realistic information base which the student can use to make an assessment of how to use the education he is receiving. In the commercial world, a good salesman does this with realism because he knows an undersold or oversold customer quickly communicates his dissatisfaction to others. Since traditional (not proprietary) higher education is likely to face a declining market for some time, good selling on the part of faculty will continue to be an important ingredient for attracting and retaining students.

Since curriculum in most schools is under the control of faculty, the faculty must also assume the role of a marketing manager. In industry a marketing manager must make the decisions about how to satisfy customer needs and wants. In curriculum development, the faculty needs to gather the hard and soft data (that is, objective studies and case analyses) which can help to lead to curricula which can be marketable in both the short and long term. This is a most difficult process, as most faculty have very specialized interests, and, in some instances, the realities of the marketplace may conflict with vested interests. Curriculum committees generally have been rather slow vehicles for change. When the professor assumes his role as a marketing manager,

<hr />

[5] E. H. Fram, "We Must Market Education," *Chronicle of Higher Education*, April 17, 1972, p. 8; and E. H. Fram, "Marketing Mismanagement in Higher Education," working paper, Rochester Institute of Technology, October 1971, pp. 11–12.

he will have to acquire a new perspective on the relationship of the curriculum product to the student buyer. In general he will have to quicken the tempo from product design to marketplace sale. In summary, a marketing philosophy in higher education proposes that faculty become salesmen and marketing managers. This two-fold responsibility requires them first to create the curricula to meet the needs of students and society, and second to be good salesmen in their contacts with student customers.

A well-executed marketing approach creates satisfied customers. The question every college or university must ask is, "What satisfies students?" The academic is only one aspect of collegiate life. Requirements for dormitories, campus social life, psychological support services, and so forth, will vary from one school to another. The recent turbulent decline of *in loco parentis* indicates that some student support services were kept beyond the period of customer need.

A marketing philosophy requires that one make it easy for the customer to buy. Colleges and universities place restraints on the buying process through admissions procedures. Businesses have been plagued by poor management preconceptions as to why customers do or do not purchase their products. The author has seen top executives use their own or their families' experiences in making value judgments about customers. Observably, the life style of an executive of a multi-million dollar or billion dollar corporation is quite different from the average family to whom he is marketing. Marketing-oriented business executives do not let preconceptions get in the way of good decision-making. The collegiate or university administrator should follow the same path and make research-based determinations about why students choose a particular school. They may find to their surprise that the academic programs are not at the top of the list in the students' decision processes. At the top may be such things as social life, geographic location, or an urban or rural environment. Although this information may be difficult for those involved with academic curricula to accept, it is valuable data for institutional planning and reform.

Some educators may feel that "current students . . . are in a sense captive customers of the university. Having decided to come to the particular university, they are largely stuck with the decision. It is not easy for them to discontinue the product or switch to another brand."[6] This point of view suggests that concepts of marketing are

---

[6] Kotler and Dubois, "A Marketing Orientation for Colleges and Universities," p. 20.

not relevant for current students. However, it ignores the great growth in numbers of transfer students, the willingness of and necessity for private institutions to accept transfers liberally, and the increasing flexibility of students in interrupting their studies at various times. As things are now developing, a marketing approach to current students will become an ever-increasing activity because the ability of the student to switch to another "supplier" is growing rapidly.

Consumer behavior is an emerging field of study within the marketing framework. Its objectives are to help the marketing man better understand the variables that cause people to purchase or fail to purchase. It would seem that higher education could move in the same direction with their student customers.

Alumni are customers who have purchased an educational product from a school. In dollar terms, each in recent years may have spent $20,000 or more for the product, and this makes it a high-priced one. On the marketing scene, high-priced products call for manufacturers' guarantees or warranties.[7] What guarantees do colleges and universities offer on their educational product? What assurance does the student have that his learning will not become obsolete quickly? A marketing viewpoint would require that educators make a continuing education provision for the student, as a guarantee that his educational package will remain viable for a reasonable length of time, considering his vocational interests. A few colleges have given lip service to continuing education, over an extended lifetime period, but few, if any, have implemented the idea.

Except for a few prestigious schools, the rate of alumni financial support has been modest. Perhaps part of the reason for this problem is that institutions of higher education offer alumni very little of significant value once the degree is earned. If alumni are considered part of one's target market, a marketing viewpoint would dictate that alumni's needs and wants be assessed in the same manner as those of anyone else associated with the academic community. (For example one college did a marketing-type readership study of its alumni publication, and changed its format completely when it found that the alumni were reading stories with pictures and ignoring stories with straight copy.) And it would seem that if the alumnus is viewed as a customer, the first need he may have is protecting from obsolescence that multithousand dollar investment in the degree purchased.

[7] Fram, "We Must Market Education," pp. 6–7; and Fram, "Marketing Mismanagement," p. 8.

A college or university does not stand alone; it is in constant interaction with people in its community. It is the natural tendency of many academicians to cloister themselves from the general community. However, recent events (especially the student riots of May 1970) clearly indicate that separation of "town from gown" is no longer an educational reality. Consequently, the college or university must market itself to those who live around it. Related to this idea is the question of image within the general community. As in the analysis of other markets discussed above, this calls for understanding of the community's image of the school as it exists, not as those within the college or university conceive it. Images are very hard to change; Kotler and Dubois showed that major changes in public images are apt to take five or ten years.[8] This writer is acquainted with one school which changed its name in 1944. Today, many older members of the community still refer to it by its pre-1944 name, and this in spite of radical changes in school program, location, and student body. If the image held by the surrounding community is a desired one, marketing techniques are available to help reinforce it. Marketing can also help if a change is required, but much time is needed. The important point is for the educator to use the tools available to make the image assessment, and this is the contribution a marketing viewpoint can make.

Integrating the marketing state of mind with the actions of business organizations has been successful where it has support from top management; it has not been a grassroots movement. Implementation of the marketing philosophy requires that plans become more precise and formal in character, and high-level support is therefore needed. Ever-present in planning is the question of hard-to-define market requirements. For institutions of higher learning too, top administration must assume certain responsibilities. It must set the style by making sure that all concerned with problems have *reasonable* (perfection is unattainable) market data on which to make decisions. This might seem like a superfluous observation for institutions which have had a long research history, but higher education itself is a poorly-researched field. Top administration needs to get faculty, administration, and students to do long-term planning—planning which must be oriented to current and future markets for education. This top support must be active; many commercial firms have found that top management talks about being marketing oriented, but by a lack of questioning and fol-

[8] Kotler and Dubois, "A Marketing Orientation," p. 29.

low-through, it allows the company to slip back into a product-oriented approach. Constant top management attention is mandatory.

In pricing the educational product the consumers must be also considered because they are the ones who will accept or reject any price.[9] In the business environment, the marketing man focuses on how the consumers perceive price. He may price some items lower because of low demand or low cost, and other items higher. He works on an averaging process (called variable pricing) over a number of items to give a reasonable return. It has been shown repeatedly that if his price becomes too high, if there is too much profit, an efficient competitor will eventually enter the market and reduce his share of the market.

Applying this principle to college and university pricing, one perceives a rigidity in pricing that may have worked against the growth of some segments of the school. Is it fair and "market wise" to charge the same price to an English major as to a chemistry major, when it costs much more (through fixed overhead) to educate the latter than the former? In reality, the English program is carrying the burden for the chemistry program! A question could be raised also about charging the same tuition for freshmen students as for senior students. The cost of educating the senior student is higher because advanced classes are smaller and more specialized.

With the financial pressures facing colleges and universities, it appears that variable pricing of tuition might present a reasonable alternative to present high education tuition. Variable pricing would provide a better balance and relate cost more realistically to demand. No doubt it would have a detrimental affect on high-priced special programs, but perhaps this is a desirable *market dictated* outcome. As a result, schools might be forced to examine realistically the cost of programs in relation to their social value.

Although many have a simplistic view that dollars invested in sales promotion automatically bring results within the marketing community, there is much debate about the ability of advertising to persuade people. For example, advertising could not have sold nonphosphate detergents ten years ago; consumers were simply not cognizant of the need for pollution control. As schools have been confronted with declining enrollment and attendant financial problems, the reaction

---

[9] Fram, "Marketing Mismanagement," pp. 5–6; and Fram, "We Must Market Education," p. 8.

of many has been to make the catalog more colorful, print slick brochures, and flood potential applicants with all types of printed materials describing the wonders of its campus. All of this is being done without asking what the best way is to reach the potential customer. A first step should be to assess current promotional approaches. How many schools have attempted a readership study of catalogs to determine what students and their *parents* have or have not read? How many schools have surveyed their student body in depth to determine why and how they arrived at the decision to register at the school, and, more appropriately, why did some students withdraw their applications? More than the simple multiple-choice questionnaire usually administered at an orientation period is required. The design of a promotional appeal for an institution of higher education goes right to the heart of the unique marketing appeal the institution has. A college or university is competing for enrollment, endowment, and grants. Customers who have the potential for associating themselves with it seek, overtly or subtly, to find a school that is different. It is up to each school to assess realistically that difference and then choose the promotional approach which best communicates it.

Educational institutions have made some very important decisions in dealing with problems of distribution—where to offer their product. The growth of community colleges, and the expansion of university opportunities via branching of various state universities illustrate the result of such decisions. New York has started the Empire State College in which a degree conceivably can be earned without attending formal classes. Adding to these opportunities are remote capabilities offered by new instructional technology. In all, the educational establishment has done well in distributing its product. Marketing techniques can be of continuing support by helping educators to better assess new locations for service.

Marketing, a method for getting the right product to the right customers at the right time, can be a useful tool for those in higher education. However, it does take planning of a different character than in the past. It is true that the marketing philosophy can be applied in only one or two areas of an institution's life, such as alumni relations or student recruitment. But results will be far greater if there is total commitment throughout a college or university. The marketing plan of business organizations can be used as a model. At the beginning, the businessman asks himself who constitutes his target markets. Marketing men have for years worked on the premise that their customers' markets, although homogeneous in appearance, are composed of a number of different subsets, or segments. For each of the segments, needs and wants are assessed. Then specific products are matched to segments and coordinated activities are established for pricing, distribution and promotion, with continual monitoring taking place while the plan is in operation. A formal marketing plan could be similarly established for higher education.

PART THREE

A Future on a
Human Scale

With the five essays of Part Three, we reach the center of the large problem to which all of this volume is devoted. The thesis that ties these essays together is also the major thesis of The Future in The Making: Of all possible futures, the only one acceptable to American educators is one in which people remain individual human beings. The only viable future for us is a future on a human scale.

In the essays of William F. Sturner and K. Patricia Cross (Chapters Nine and Ten) which open Part Three, the prospect is relatively optimistic. Sturner shows how it is indeed possible to humanize the physical attributes of a campus. He presents for our inspection a detailed picture of a campus that has an organic relationship to student and faculty growth, and we can feel that such a campus is well within the grasp of the next generation of campus planners. Cross's essay also leaves us with a positive and achievable goal. She shows us how institutional diversity can meet the needs of students in the years *to come, and she suggests that the needed reforms can take place within the established framework of American higher education.*

Hugh W. Lane, however, introduces a note of pessimisim in his essay (Chapter Eleven). He asks us first to look at what has happened in the past to those segments of our college-age population that were not white, or not of Northern European origin, or not of Protestant background, or not male. If we then gauge the progress of the past twenty years (for it is almost two decades since the famous Supreme Court decision of 1954), we find it difficult to be cheerful about the future.

A bit of optimism may return to some readers as Valentine Rossilli Winsey presents in her essay (Chapter Twelve) a sensible and enthusiastic argument in favor of a radically new concept of organizing higher education along interdisciplinary lines. But the pessimism will surely remain for those who believe that the established pattern of curricular fragmentation is too well entrenched to accommodate the reorganization that Winsey envisions.

We come, then, to the final chapter of Part Three, which offers a choice between pessimism and optimism—and it will undoubtedly leave the reader unsettled. In the essay by Dennis L. Meadows and Lewis Perelman (Chapter Thirteen), we are presented with two— and only two—alternative futures. We can have, according to these authors, an end to anything resembling human civilization or we can create an entirely new kind of civilization. The new civilization can be developed, however, under only one condition: our educational establishment must be prepared, from top to bottom, to reeducate its own members and they, in turn, must devote themselves to reeducating the whole society. The authors believe that the second alternative is still within the realm of possibility, but they warn that the human race cannot delay much longer. In spite of the technical language of this essay, the reader will find its power overwhelming.

JOSEPH AXELROD

9

The College Environment

William F. Sturner

The sizes and shapes of buildings are important. So are the landscaping and the contours of walkways and roads. Individually or in combination, the physical attributes of a university express the character and temperament of that institution. They also have a direct impact on the effectiveness of the learning process.[1] It should not be surprising to anyone that the style, color, and arrangement of the architecture and landscaping give a campus a physiognomy, a set of traits which communicates the personality of the institution and its

[1] The concept and theory of behavior settings and ecological environments are treated in Roger Barker, *Ecological Psychology* (Stanford: Stanford University Press, 1968); George Stern, "Self-actualizing Environments for Students," *School Review* (November 1971), pp. 1–25; and Seymour B. Sarason, *The Creation of Settings and the Future Societies* (San Francisco: Jossey-Bass, 1972).

inhabitants. This is true of almost all inanimate extensions of man. A tennis racket and sneakers, for example, suggest an urge for informality and exertion. Golf clubs are shaped both for accuracy and pleasure. A horse mounted for the fox hunt stirs very different emotions from one harnessed for the plow.

In the same way, a campus of broad and straight lines reflects an accent on order, on processions, on the search for uncluttered truth. The dominance of three-story, block-like buildings on straight streets connotes a premium on efficiency at the expense of imaginative links with the earth or the sky. The formal appearance of a library with its potted plants, rows of books and all-pervasive coding system usually suggests a cerebral greenhouse devoted to abstracted thought in repose. And the presence on campus of covered pathways, curved and narrow streets, bright and varying colors, playing fields, and streams and fountains, reflect a tactile experience of process, motion, and vitality.

A catalog with its list of courses and calendars and credentials tells a prospective student very little about a school's style and pace of living. This is why many students and their parents intuitively know enough to visit the campus before making decisions, to witness its environment, to inspect the noncurricular atmosphere, to take an inventory of stimuli, to gain a feeling for the institution.

And universities have markedly different atmospheres. The physical setting of Columbia University, for example, is an expression of the desires of the faculty and students as modified by the realities of New York City—congested, noisy, and complex, dotted with large buildings and crowded walkways, attempting to serve both those who walk with prancing poodles on Morningside Heights and those who emerge from the swirling humanity of Harlem. The dignity and elegance of Rice University is a testimony to the goals of its benefactors, the aspirations of its students, and the financial accomplishments of the residents of Houston, just as the quaint, intimate, and rustic setting of Bowdoin College mirrors the style and preoccupations of a small but lively college town off the coast of Maine.

The planned development of a suburban campus by the State University Center in Buffalo reflects an urge to relate to the characteristics of the growing suburban population in Erie county. The decision to supplement the old buildings and temporary structures in Buffalo with the new campus in Amherst may give to SUNY Buffalo a size, shape, and image that will better reflect its goals of eminence and influence. The magnificent murals, the large outdoor swimming facilities, and the constant flow of people at the National Autonomous University in Mexico City express an educational process which is open, restless, and fluid. The lovely architecture of the University of Washington in Seattle, and the beautiful setting of the University of Wisconsin in Madison, are manifestations of academic prestige; the aura of restrained elegance pervading both campuses may also be the reason why some radical students spent so much time attempting to deface the symbols of a way of life they wished to replace.

More importantly, the physical environment of the university not only expresses values and activities, but is their determinant as well; the iconographic characteristics of a campus are significant be cause they not only reflect, but form a framework for, a way of life. There is a good deal of wisdom in the aphorism, usually attributed to Winston Churchill, that "as we shape our buildings, so they shape us."[2] The interior design of buildings, the style and contour of the external architecture, and the layout and landscaping of the space between buildings can stimulate or depress, expand or contract the learning process. Individually or in concert, the physical components of a university can complement a curriculum or neutralize it. They can give witness to a philosophy of education or undercut the intentions or accomplishments of the faculty. In short, the role of the physical environment in which learning takes place is integrally related to the educational objectives of an institution. In the words of Bernard Rudofsky, the classroom, like the street, "cannot exist in a vacuum, it is inseparable from its environment . . . it is no better than the company of houses it keeps . . . its viability depends as much on the right kind of architecture as on the right kind of humanity."[3]

These are simple truths. Judging from the look and sound and feel of many colleges, however, it seems that the role of the physical environment in the educational process is being sorely neglected. Buildings and courses do not seem to be related; pedagogy and the size, shape, and contour of the campus are not intertwined. The classroom appears to be suspended in a vacuum, divorced from the many other components of an integrated learning environment.

[2] Theodore Larson (director), SER: *School Environments Research* (Ann Arbor: Architectural Research Laboratory, University of Michigan, 1965), Volume III, p. i.
[3] Bernard Rudofsky, *Streets for People* (Garden City, N.Y.: Doubleday, 1969), p. 20.

It is difficult to point to specific portions of a university setting which close off or engender stimulation, or which give it a distinctive stamp, since the experience of one's environment is usually a matter of a total field experience. "Environments are invisible," writes Marshall McLuhan. "Their ground rules, pervasive structures, and overall patterns elude easy perception."[4] There are particular features, however, which create the impression of austerity and finality versus warmth and involvement. Signs and shapes and enclosed spaces which indicate variations on the theme of *stop, keep off the grass, detour, this means you,* are discouragements to participation, both physically and mentally. Campuses planned without alternatives for individualized thoughts or actions, which arbitrarily determine the type and shape of stimuli (like painting by numbers), stifle individual explorations and the free encounter of persons and things.

There are many campuses which fail to capitalize on, and sometimes even destroy, the desire of people to identify with their surroundings, to leave their imprint on the environment through use and personal memory. Insensitivity and malfeasance often blend to produce such roadblocks to the imagination as rectangular buildings with sharp corners and no details or surprises, the dominance of straight roads intersecting two dots, a campus built around streets and highways which permit and even encourage speedy entrance and exit, an environment which is all horizontal or all vertical, and the absence of flower beds and wild flowers and flowing water and kites and covered paths and secluded places and public squares and variations in food, flora, and fauna.

Too often the residents of a campus are confronted with such fabricated abnormalities as walkways which conflict with the natural walkings patterns of the users and which are cluttered with fences and chains and signs, the destruction of trees for new foundations, that slick, clean, impersonal look which prevents the evolution of landmarks or memorials with which to identify, a cold mood of completion and finality which keeps the residents at arms-length and assures that they will remain spectators, the hegemony of abstract master plans which grind on to completion without consent or consultation.[5]

---

[4] Marshall McLuhan, *The Medium is the Message: An Inventory of Effects* (New York: Bantam, 1967), pp. 84–85.

[5] Colleges and universities, of course, have no monopoly on such environmental problems. A good example of similar laments about the urban environment is William H. Whyte's "Please, Just A Nice Place To Sit: A Tough

As a consequence of such errors of judgment and taste, many college campuses have about the same appeal as the local museum or the library stacks. Unlike the personalized rooms in the dormitory, or the common living areas which literally reflect their name through constant use and activity, many campus buildings, classrooms, and roadways lack the quality of warmth. Their forbidding, highly-defined and austere appearance does not invite participation. They do not excite, or surprise, or stimulate the senses. In short, too few campuses offer an invitation to their users to develop a sense of place on campus; too few have physiognomies which encourage a symbiotic and evolutionary interaction between the residents and their physical surroundings.

The reasons why many campuses are unexciting and drab are easy to understand. Most members of the university community—faculty, staff and students alike—are insensitive or simply don't care, unconsciously tolerating arid environments because such austerity complements the rational, visual, and linear thrust of their book-oriented lives. There are, of course, many others who yearn for an all-encompassing relationship with the physical setting and the experience of communal participation in the use and fulfillment of the campus. These are the people who feel the gap between the actual and the possible but who, because of busy calendars, or lack of energy, or an inability to communicate the essence of something at once so obvious and yet so subtle, concede decision-making on campus development to the relatively aggressive and possessive work habits of developers and engineers. But sensitivity to what a university is, or what a given grouping of faculty and staff and students hopes to accomplish, does not come naturally to the many technically trained people who plan and develop our campuses—an understandable situation in view of the general indifference and passivity of even those who use the campus. The source of the problem, then, at least in the eyes of those who would make the campus a tactile encounter of the entire sensorium, is the merging of rational indifference with the efficient but myopic approach of the technician. The result inevitably is a one-dimensional visual campus, logical, antiseptic, and without life.

Town For Shmoozing," *New York Times Magazine,* December 3, 1972, pp. 20ff. An excellent assessment of the impact of progress on the city of London, which I think is applicable to all types of environmental settings, is explored by Lynn Langway and Jerry Edgerton, "The Inevitable Question Comes To Piccadilly: In Which Direction Does Progress Lie?," *New York Times* (Travel and Resorts Section), July 16, 1972, pp. 1ff.

Both the process and the product must be changed, however, if the university is to provide the stimulating sense of place essential to the development of an understanding of self and others. What is needed are physical environments at our colleges and universities which both reflect and stimulate the age-old yearning for organic relationships, communal involvements, and wraparound experiences. These goals can only be attained if the institution becomes a tangible expression of the life styles, interests, and aspirations of its residents—if the students, faculty, and staff are involved in the evolution of the very shapes and forms that envelop them.

In other words, the use to which materials are put at a university should be guided by the fact that a university—unlike a recreation center, hospital, or factory—is concerned with the exploration and implementation of ideas, the search for identity, and the interaction of individuals in a community of thinking activists. The environment of a university must relate to and support the educational experience, that dynamic process in which persons spend several years questioning, challenging, building, and, moreover, seeking encounters in and of the world of people and things.

What, then, are the standards for building a physical environment which expresses the essence of the university? What environmental code or set of principles should guide the deployment of materials so as to facilitate the search for the understanding of self and others?

(1) Steen Eiler Rasmussen has called for a "human scale," since "architecture means shapes formed around man, formed to be lived in, not merely . . . seen from the outside."[6] In this view, the evolution of a campus environment must be based on an assessment of what individuals actually experience on campus, and not on what armchair planners think is a good idea. One could periodically plot the path and thus survey the sensory exposures of varying types of inhabitants in the course of a day or week. The path and thus the activities, opportunities, and exposures of some resident students, for example, might be very different from those of certain commuters. The disparity between the actual experience and the projected needs and interests of each would then determine how the university should recreate its environment.

(2) A university should be guided by a philosophy of education which helps "each student to develop, to the highest degree pos-

[6] Steen Eiler Rasmussen, *Experiencing Architecture* (Cambridge, Mass.: M.I.T. Press, 1962), p. 10.

sible, a rich and varied impulse life, as well as a repertory of intellectual skills and abilities."[7] Thus the campus must be a tactile experience, one which tickles all of the senses. Its design should not be visual only, but should invite connections with the ear through various acoustical reverberations, with the hand and foot through variations in temperature, texture, and level, and with the nose through the scent of books, kitchens, and flowers.

(3) The campus environment should be developed in the vernacular, expressing and extending the characteristics indigenous to the native area, population, or culture.[8] New York University should and does reflect the unique locale of Greenwich Village just as the style, location, and contour of the college houses at Santa Cruz express the search for community amidst the expanse of hills and trees. "People want to feel that they can shape their own personal environment," writes Moshe Safdie, that "they can change it, they can choose it, and that it is not imposed on them, and they like to feel that it is not the same as everybody else's because they are not the same as other people. In fact, the ideal would be dwellings [campuses] that are as different from each other as human faces and personalities are different from each other."[9]

(4) The environment must not be too "hot," determined, finished, or overwhelming in its details. Only in the actual day-to-day participation in the building of his habitat does man identify with it, with all of its attendant stimulants and allegiances. The environment must remain malleable and in process in order to invite participation in its perfection. The campus, like the curriculum, must give each generation of students, staff, and faculty the opportunity to create, not just absorb or consume. "In contrast to the rest of creation," Ortega y Gasset reminds us, "man, in existing, has to make his existence. He has to solve the practical problem of transferring into reality the program that is himself. For this reason my life is pure task, a thing inexorably to be made."[10]

---

[7] Joseph Axelrod and others, *Search for Relevance* (San Francisco: Jossey-Bass, 1969), p. 26.

[8] The great exponent of cooperating with the natural habitat is, of course, Ian L. McHarg, *Design With Nature* (Garden City, N.Y.: Natural History Press), 1969.

[9] Moshe Safdie, *Beyond Habitat* (Cambridge, Mass.: M.I.T. Press, 1970), pp. 150–151.

[10] Quoted in Marshall McLuhan, *War and Peace in a Global Village* (New York: Bantam, 1968), p. 176.

(5) The only way that the physical environment of the university can complement the formal learning process and represent the accomplishments and aspirations of its inhabitants is to institutionalize the inputs of the residents. An all-university committee, composed of representatives of the students, faculty, and staff, in addition to the president (and the planning officers, construction engineers, and landscape architects), should be formed to consider and make recommendations on all policies which affect both the long-range aspects of campus planning and the short-range issues of construction, maintenance, landscaping, and conservation.

Inclusion on such a committee would not guarantee that all inhabitants would be interested and sensitive, or that all decisions would favor the particular interests of specific groups. It would insure, however, that those who used the campus had an institutionalized mechanism by which to foster their own enthusiasm, and simultaneously modify, where necessary, the perspective of planners, architects, and engineers. Committee goals would be, first, to sensitize the inhabitants; second, to recondition the sensibilities of the professionals in the hope that they too will treat each component of the environment as an integral portion of the total university; and third, to facilitate a mutually supporting relationship between the users and the technicians.

Thus architecture would not be viewed as expressive of the designer, but as a functional and psychic manifestation of the meaning of the university and the accomplishments and aspirations of a particular community of thinking-activists. The builder would also maintain his discretion, but he too would become the instrument for implementing the vernacular. Textiles, graphics, furniture, flowers, and other manifestations of the work and experience of students, faculty, and staff, could then be woven into a true habitat for learning formed by, for, and of the community.

(6) Out of these principles and approaches should emerge not only a collection of forms and shapes, but an integrated physical environment that both reflects and generates that rhythmic sense of place associated with a particular set of university students and their tutors.

Both these standards and these practices continue to gain acceptance at more and more colleges and universities. As an extension of the general interest in ecology, groups of students, faculty and staff have discovered that the quality of life on campus has been undercut by devastation, by neglect, and by insensitive planning of classrooms, buildings, recreational areas, roadways, and the landscape.[11] Growing concern for the total habitat of the university has dramatized the role that the physical environment can and should play in supporting the living-learning process. It also has demonstrated that personal involvement in the creative but relatively inexpensive construction of one's own habitat can be very gratifying. The process of creation, in short, has the potential to become personalized. The power to reflect on the need for a compatible environment, to make recommendations based on one's own experiential encounters with the physical world, to work together with receptive engineers, architects and planners, has helped to resurrect a sense of place on many college campuses. And because it has become personal, the process has involved the investment of more individual time and less institutional money.

An excellent example of this transformation in process and in product has been Oakland University, in Rochester, Michigan.[12] Oakland was created thirteen years ago as a result of a gift by Mrs. Matilda Dodge Wilson of sixteen hundred acres of wooded land and rolling hills in southeast Michigan. By 1969, the northwest corner of some 165 acres had been developed as the main site of the campus and housed some fifty million dollars worth of new bricks and mortar. Aside from the few acres surrounding the original estate and manor home of Mr. and Mrs. John Dodge, and the building of a pavilion for the Meadow Brook Music Festival, the remainder of the land was still in its natural state.[13]

[11] See, for example, "Physical and Psychological Environments Polluted by Colleges, Health Group Is Told," *The Chronicle of Higher Education,* May 17, 1971, p. 5, summarizing the viewpoints of a number of students, educators, and administrators.

[12] Numerous other examples, perhaps more illustrative, exist but not enough detail is known about them at this time to attempt a similar case study. The most recent to come to the attention of this author is the Green Committee, composed of volunteer community members who have set about the task of improving or "greening" the environment of Harvard University. Similar groups were much in evidence at scores of institutions during the period of ecological emphasis on campus between 1968 and 1972. Whether the momentum of the initial community concern has been sustained at particular institutions, I do not know at this writing.

[13] Oakland University has been the subject of several analyses by David Riesman of Harvard University. His studies, however, have focused primarily on the development and interaction of the faculty, the student body, and the curriculum of the university, and have not attempted to examine the physical environment of Oakland as either a cause or an effect of its formal institutional profile. See, for example, his *Academic Values and Mass Education* (New York:

But there were problems. In the opinion of many, the campus was relatively barren: the buildings were nondescript, the landscaping drab and forbidding, the roadways poorly planned, and the design, texture, and appearance of building interiors bland and unattractive. Most of the original barns, which once had housed the Wilson stables, had been torn down and replaced by modern but relatively antiseptic structures. Utility companies had scarred the land through the installation of public sewer and power lines which criss-crossed the length and width of the sixteen hundred-acre campus.

Many felt that the large "back" or wooded areas were separated from the campus by an invisible cordon; there was no linkage or relationship between the two since the university faced towards the roads and highways that serviced it and not toward the land that was its greatest resource. Situated nine miles east of Pontiac and five miles west of Rochester, with little of interest in between, the university was also landlocked—it was neither inviting to nor invited by the outside community. The residence hall students, in particular, were deprived of access to the glitter, the mystique, and the stimulus of off-campus congregations of people involved in living-learning activities far different from those emphasized in a university setting.

The main difficulty was that the operative educational mission of the university was limited primarily to excellence in the verbalization and transcription of information. The physical environment mirrored this emphasis and accordingly was allowed to draw inward to complement the no-nonsense dedication to book learning. The unique and homey setting of the Dodge farm—with scores of barns and fences and fixtures—was destroyed to make way for box-like buildings on a placid, unimaginative campus. The horses and ponies and pigs and sheep were moved to the preserves of the relatively small Wilson estate on the other side of the campus, where the distinctive farm-manor environment was maintained but was not linked to or accessible to the academic community on the other side of the university's property. The cerebral approach was also reflected in the fact that courses in physical education were not offered; athletics were tolerated but not in the form of intercollegiate contacts; trees and shrubs and flowers were scarce; classrooms and offices and hallways were barren except for books; and the landscaping was more functional than aesthetic,

Doubleday, 1970), written in conjunction with Joseph Gusfield and Zelda Gamson.

confined more to maintenance than the molding of an all-encompassing habitat.

Having failed initially to realize the enormous potential for a more expressive, multifaceted and tactile educational environment, deprived of mental and physical access to the surrounding communities and with its back to its hills and streams and trees, the university shackled its nervous system and stunted the educational enterprise. An apt caricature might have depicted the university at that stage in its development as a person with a huge cranium, large eyes fixed in a myopic stare, an enormous mouth, tiny ears, hands, and legs, and the smallest of bodies.

But things changed and rather rapidly, reflecting new currents both in the university's use of its environment and in its philosophy of education. The mutual interaction between the two was apparent. The effect was to foster the growth of a more inclusive environment, one that could be felt and heard as well as seen. Concurrently, university programs evolved to incorporate service externships in the surrounding communities, a series of applied programs in education, management, and engineering, and many new student-life activities focused in and around the residence halls and a new student center.

Beginning in the fall of 1969, a group of ten students, faculty, and staff banded together, first as a Long-Range Development Committee, and subsequently as the Campus Development Committee (both of the University Senate), and set about the task of improving the quality of life on campus. Prodded by an interest in ecology, riding the crest of a series of programmatic changes in many areas of the university, and driven by the need to stop further inroads on the quality of the land, this small group provided impetus for a renewed interest in a more expansive and expressive concept of an educational environment.

Through a series of reports, recommendations, confrontations, and do-it-yourself activities, the group was able to get a number of people to invest their sensitivities and their time. Little in the way of institutional funding was necessary. In other words, the committee's credo was not to spend more on grandiose schemes, but to get the total community, working with the professional staff of the physical plant department, to complete dozens of relatively small and inexpensive projects of significance.

In the course of the next four years, given the energy and insight of the original committee and its successors and the forceful leadership provided by Glen Brown, the newly-appointed assistant president for campus development, the environment at Oakland University was transformed from a state of neglect to one possessing the elements of a quality habitat for learning.

A unique cluster of barns, sheds, and old rural fences and fixtures, once used to house and care for horses, sheep and cows, were saved from destruction, and was subsequently designated as "The Village." One of the barns, converted a few years before by student carpenters and electricians into a Student Enterprise Theatre, became the base of operations. A former creamery was converted into offices; a Belgian Barn was revamped to house the university carpentry shop; a long, L-shaped, former animal shed was stabilized and reshaped for the motor pool; and a remaining barn is now slated for conversion into a combination gallery, flea-market, and student activities center. The old stone fences, lighting fixtures, and stone foundations of barns razed earlier are now planned as the future home of an outdoor sculpture garden and combined meeting and picnic area. Two acres of land adjacent to the building will become either a park or a student farm.[14]

The installation of a public water line by a local utility company was scheduled for the fall of 1970 to traverse the length of the campus, cutting a swath of some two hundred feet through the tree lines, and disturbing and perhaps destroying streams, swamps, and the gentle flow of the hills. The contract would have been consummated except for the loud protests of the committee members. The water line was eventually installed by, but not on or through, university property. A series of trails were planned to acquaint members of the community with various plants, trees, and terrain available on the campus. The trails are also being used to preserve the land bounded by them as a nature area and an arboretum, both to be used to support various programs in ecology.

The most far-reaching set of recommendations came in the

14 The many colleges and universities which have undertaken similar remodeling and renovation projects of this sort have thereby conserved areas of charm and character for a relatively modest outlay of funds. See "Sourcebook on Modernization," published by *College and University Business,* Chicago, Illinois, 1971; "Renovating Old Buildings Called Often Wiser For Colleges Than Erecting New Ones," *The Chronicle of Higher Education,* April 12, 1971, p. 6; "Remodeling," *College and University Business,* June 1971, pp. 42ff; and "New Campuses of Old Buildings," *College Management,* November 1970, pp. 8ff.

form of an "Aesthetic Accouterments Report."[15] Written by two students and two staff members, the report listed "those things—accouterments—which would enhance . . . life on campus" by providing "more variety in shapes, textures, sizes and colors."

The recommendations were drawn up in accordance with the following guidelines: (1) to create tradition and campus lore through campus development; (2) to relate developments in continuity to an over-all campus plan; (3) to produce imaginative, creative links between people and the components of the physical environment; (4) to provide inexpensive approaches because big money was not available and waiting for it to accumulate was destructive of momentum, morale, and the maintenance of a personal stake in improvements; (5) to produce a variety of aesthetic and psychological experiences to complement or facilitate the varied moods and interests of people living and learning in an academic community; and (6) to add, in a material way, something audial, visual, or tactile to the university environment.

Most of the recommendations provided by the Subcommittee on Accouterments have now become a reality because of the dedication of a host of faculty, students, and administrators, and the commitment of the university's staff of professional engineers and landscapers. As recommended, dozens of trees and numerous flower beds, all grown in the university nursery, have been planted throughout the campus. Shrubs have replaced chain fences. Wood chips and crushed stone are being used more frequently as alternatives to asphalt and concrete. Wooden benches were installed along the pathways. The shorelines of the numerous creeks on campus were restored and maintained. Bridges over the creeks were repaired and made usable for foot traffic. Walkways were contoured and where possible were redirected to bring the stroller alternatively in view of flowers, and vistas, and congregations of people. Large rocks and boulders were set out for sitting, painting, and climbing. Swings were erected. Outdoor basketball courts were cleared. A soccer field was completed inside an outdoor running track. The baseball diamond was sodded and the field was provided

[15] *Report of the Aesthetic Accouterments Committee,* a subcommittee of the Long-Range Development Committee, William Betts, Allan Chamberlin, William Marshall (chairman), and William Sturner. Oakland University, October 1971 (unpublished).

a fenced-in backstop. A drinking fountain was installed near the tennis courts!

Students opened a farm coop. Campus ecology teams repaired lake and river banks, renovated old buildings, and gathered and removed trash and debris. A professor planted pumpkins and sunflowers outside his first-floor office. Students organized an outdoor photo-and-apple show. Roads that intersected the campus were closed off and the resultant peripheral road system allowed the entire campus to become a pedestrian mall. Barns were painted. Dumping on the back campus was stopped. Soil erosion was controlled through plantings.

A multitude of old and unused signs and directional signals were removed. Rooms and corridors were repainted in bright and pastel colors. Large stone remnants of Mrs. Wilson's magnificent and unique gazebo were placed throughout the campus—to stimulate curiosity and provide a link to the past. A "Campus Detail Study" was completed by a professional firm; it now serves as a guide to the university landscape architects in their campaign to plant particular trees and shrubs and flowers in certain clusters and in specific areas so as to enhance the stimulative value, the beauty, and the flavor of the campus.

Other suggestions that have not yet been implemented are either in process or under serious consideration. And of course, the Office of Campus Development and its advisory committees continue to generate ideas for perfecting the environment. For example, university officials have met with the district soil conservationist and other state and federal officials and have sought their counsel on water control, soil control, woodlot management, wildlife conservation, and natural resources management. Small parks are in the planning stage to provide opportunities for meditation, study, courtship, or just sitting. Student study and congregation areas had never been provided in campus buildings, so some classrooms and offices are now slated for conversion into lounges. Furniture in L-shape placement will be set up in some hallways to encourage use of the corridors as something other than conduits.

The campus has a small lake near the residence hall area, and streams running through the back property, but there are no decorative fountains, pools, water geysers, or other evidence of the beauty and movement of water on campus. However, a fountain given to the university ten years ago was discovered in the basement of the library.

It is now slated for installation, probably somewhere in the vicinity of the student center.

A huge metal bell, used to celebrate at the annual birthday party held for Mrs. Wilson, has been in disuse since her death four years ago. A permanent site for the bell would give the campus an added symbol of tradition. The names of university streets and roads are repetitious and without experiential significance to most students or users of the campus. A movement to allow the students and staff to choose labels more fitting to a university and particularly to Oakland University has been launched.

The planting of a seedling or a stock tree to celebrate the birth of a child born to any faculty, student, or staff member has been suggested. A small plaque commemorating the occasion could be installed as well. Plaques describing the variety of all trees on campus would provide a point of interest en route to classes. Sundials, birdhouses, fruit trees, a campfire site, ivy, campus maps showing present and projected usage—all would provide stimulating links to the community of people and things, and at very moderate costs.

Classrooms need to be transformed from echo chambers and human storage bins into living areas. Drawings, maps, an ongoing chronological record of class activities, tack boards, bright colors, and moveable furniture would allow the classroom to become animated, a natural extension of the human drama that unfolds there. Students and faculty are also becoming more involved in the planning of new buildings in the hope that the exterior architecture and the interior design will more aptly reflect the intended use and user. A bus system, linking the university to the surrounding communities, is planned. Commercial development on the periphery of the campus of curio shops, beer halls, groceries, pizza parlors, and theatres is being encouraged by university officials.[16]

Concepts that will guide the long-range development of the physical campus have been reviewed and approved by the board of trustees.[17] They include a dedication to the maintenance of the central campus as a pedestrian mall and the perfection of a peripheral road

[16] A number of other suggestions are outlined in my article "University Code: Creating a Sense of Place on the College Campus," *Journal of Higher Education,* February 1972, pp. 97–109.

[17] *Guidelines for Continuing Physical Development: Oakland University,* by Johnson, Johnson and Roy, Ann Arbor, Michigan, January 1971.

system. The board also thought it wise to accommodate the growing student body (8100 in the winter, 1972) through increasing the density of building on the present campus site before expanding to the other buildable plateaus on the back property. This approach will allow the university to absorb modest growth and expansion, as it is necessary, through increased utilization, rather than by destruction of the trees and hills and streams and wildlife which make up the remaining twelve hundred acres.

The approach and the goals are clear: the inhabitants of a university want and need the psychic support of a stimulating environment. Just as one seeks sustenance at home by creating living areas that extend individual or family interests onto the walls and floors and windows, so do persons in their roles on campus need to build habitats which both express and support the activities of growth and discovery. The happenings at Oakland and elsewhere also dramatize the potential for creating such stimulative and tactile environments without large investments of money. Sensitivity, cooperation, investment of personal energy, and the commitment to respond to the intended user are the key ingredients. The rewards of such community effort are enormous. The reflections and reverberations produced by one's own constructs can generate ever-widening circles of interaction. Identity can be created with things and ideas but especially with the exploratory processes which enliven them. Moreover, learning environments orchestrated by the inhabitants produce experiences and structures which are self-generating. Icons simply function more effectively than straight roads and have a more lasting impact.

☙ 10 ☙

New Students in a New World

K. Patricia Cross

Higher education faces a profound crisis of purpose. Only a few short years ago, higher education was giving full allegiance to the goal of academic excellence. Selective admissions became a skilled operation nationally as well as on local campuses. Talent searches were launched to seek out the academically gifted, and scholarships were awarded to those who could demonstrate that they were already among the best educated young people in the nation. Institutional success was measured along narrow dimensions of academic excellence—by mean SAT scores, number of National Merit Scholars, percentage of students entering graduate schools, number and size of research grants, and the scholarly productivity of the faculty. We were remarkably effective in creating a system of higher education that pursued the goal of academic excellence with enthusiasm and effectiveness. We provided the nation with a brain trust that could compete with that of any country in the world. And the engineers and businessmen that we graduated led us to unprecedented scientific achievement and the production of material necessities and luxuries undreamed of by previous generations.

Is it any wonder that we are thrown into a period of confusion and adjustment when the nation seems to say, Stop, you have done your job too well. Supply has outstripped demand. For the present, at least, we have too many teachers, too many graduate students, too much emphasis on science and technology. Furthermore, you've selected the mosts privileged young people, added the full benefits of a remarkable advanced education to their advantages, and in so doing have created an intolerable gap between the haves and the have nots.

We are now asked not only to stop what we have learned to do so well, but to turn around and see how fast we can make progress in the opposite direction. We are now to give our attention not to the academically gifted, but to the educationally disadvantaged. Money is available for remedial education, but not for graduate study. Financial assistance to students is to be based on need, not on academic ability. Faculty members are to give more attention to teaching and less to research.

These pressures for change are not random or unrelated. Rather they are the visible elements of an underlying change in the purpose of postsecondary education. In the 1950s and early 1960s, a basic purpose of higher education was to provide the nation with a cadre of leaders who would use their advanced training for invention, production, and the advancement of knowledge that would raise the standard of living throughout the country. Our need now is not so much for further invention and production as for better distribution systems, more broadly-based education, and more concern for individuals. The way to improve life for everyone is no longer to educate a few for positions of leadership but rather to educate the masses to their full humanity.

Although higher education was never designed to educate the masses, and there are those who contend that it should not be, events have moved beyond that debate. Most high school graduates now enter college. In fact the proportion of students entering college from the upper academic half of the high school graduating classes is now so high—over 75 percent—that there are not many academically well-prepared students left to recruit from any strata of society.

A group of young people whom we used to dismiss as "not college material" are now walking through the open doors of colleges, and they constitute a growing proportion of the college population. Numerically, most of the students graduating in the lowest academic third of the high school classes are not ethnic minorities but rather are the low-achieving white sons and daughters of blue-collar workers. For one reason or another, these students have not done well in school; they are students who by definition are not prepared to do college work.

To date, our fairly simplistic solution has been to establish remedial programs in the hope that we can get these students ready to perform the standard academic tasks that constitute our concept of a college education. We have concentrated on changing students to fit what we have to offer without seriously engaging the question of whether the "ability to do college work" as it is presently defined is the measure of the best education that we can offer to these and other students.

According to some recent research, there are widespread feelings that the standard college learning experiences are not the best education that we can devise. Last spring, Richard Peterson, of Educational Testing Service, undertook a study for the Joint Committee on the Master Plan for Higher Education of the California State Legislature. In this research, he administered the Institutional Goals Inventory (IGI) to faculty, students, administrators, trustees, and citizens of the local communities of 116 private and public colleges in California. Each group was asked to rate their college as it *is* and as it *should be* on twenty different institutional goals.

Experience with *is* and *should be* ratings is that respondents almost always think the institution should be doing better than it is in absolute terms. Peterson's comparisons, however, are *rankings* which indicate the importance of goals relative to one another. The data show that students on every type of campus agree that the present emphasis on the acquisition of knowledge in the academic disciplines is overemphasized relative to other important goals. Students in the community colleges, state colleges, and private colleges of California say that emphasis on academic development ranks first in importance on their campus, whereas it should rank somewhere down in the middle in the list of twenty goals. Undergraduates at seven University of California campuses think the acquisition of academic knowledge is overdone, too, but they say that research and advanced graduate and professional training is given even more attention. If they had their way, university students would place academic development fourteenth in the list of twenty goals. We do have an identity problem when students across the spectrum of academic ability give our major activity such low priority.

Their rejection, however, should not be interpreted as anti-intellectualism. Students are strongly supportive of activities that place more emphasis on the development of the appreciations and skills of learning. They recognize as important goals such as these: instilling a commitment to lifelong learning, creating the desire for self-directed learning, and developing in students the skills of analysis and synthesis. Significantly, faculty, administrators, and trustees agree with students; they too would like to deemphasize the acquisition of knowledge in favor of stressing the utilization and appreciation of learning.

The IGI data indicate that there is widespread recognition that the cart has run away with the horse—that the academic disciplines have become the end rather than the means to quality education. With the explosion of knowledge and the realization that facts and information learned in college will not last even a decade beyond graduation, a shift from the acquisition of knowledge to the development of learning skills and appreciations should be one of our top priorities. The difficulty, of course, is that no one knows how to teach appreciations and attitudes very well. But it must be admitted that we have placed a lot of obstacles in the way of our finding out. We might start to seek some answers, for example, by questioning the sacred assumption that higher education should be organized around academic departments. It is said that had the Edsel been an academic department it would be with us yet.

In decrying the emphasis on the academic disciplines, I am not suggesting that students can learn to think in the absence of anything to think about. But I am suggesting that intellectual enquiry implies that we start with problems and seek information that helps in their solution, rather than starting with the information and hoping for a problem that can put to use what we have learned. Problems, it seems, are found all around us—within academic disciplines, across academic disciplines, under the hood of an automobile, in the health needs of the poor, and in the library of the scholar. Equal educational opportunity does not mean that all students are exposed to a standard body of information, but that each individual is helped to develop the capabilities to solve the problems that are of importance to him or her.

A good place to start problem-oriented learning is with the problems that are of concern to college students. The students in Peterson's California goals study showed extensive dissatisfaction with the lack of attention presently given to the personal development of students. Students on all types of campuses agreed that colleges should give the goal of student development top priority. But the students enrolled in community and private colleges gave their institutions higher marks for accomplishment of this goal than did students at state colleges and universities. Students on university campuses, for example, say that the goal of helping students to develop as people presently ranks eighteenth in the list of twenty goals, whereas it should rank fourth in importance. Unfortunately, the university is not likely to do much about student wishes for reform in this area. The power structure of the university—faculty, administrators, and regents—indicate on the IGI that there are many things they think more important than student development.

The community colleges and private colleges, on the other hand, can marshall substantial support among their faculty, administrators, and trustees for a strong emphasis on the non-cognitive aspects of learning. Historically, many private colleges have built a reputation as intimate communities offering a high degree of personal attention. But the very high interest of the community college faculties and administrators in student development is an encouraging sign of the willingness of public higher education to accommodate the developmental needs of students. It is sometimes hard to know, of course, what people have in mind when they endorse a goal of student development. The IGI defines it quite specifically as helping students to do the following things: identify and pursue the accomplishment of their personal goals, develop a sense of self-worth and self-confidence, achieve deeper levels of self-understanding, and develop open and trusting relationships with others. It is these goal statements that the community college faculties are accepting as part of their responsibility.

Given such encouraging support, however, the question arises as to how we go about accomplishing these goals. Traditional higher education doesn't have much experience in establishing the kinds of programs that are designed to help people become better and happier human beings. Student development is not something that can be left to the counseling staff. The development of self-confidence and a sense of self-worth, for example, are major problems for many community college students. I suspect that the most realistic path to self-confidence consists of succeeding at tasks that are worth doing. Establishing the tasks of education and setting the standards for performance are the responsibility of the total educational community, and not the counselors alone.

.I doubt that we can work effectively toward the personal development of students without permitting them to work and study in the fields in which they have some realistic hope of excelling. Traditional college students have always done well in school, and evaluation of performance along narrow dimensions of traditional academic education has not done great harm to their sense of self-confidence and self-esteem. But students who are in college today only because of open door admissions practices have always been below-average performers in school—and society permits young people no other occupation. Thus it has been extremely difficult for these students to discover special talents, let alone develop them. Until we can get away from emphasizing only two of the known human talents—verbal and quantitative skills—we are not likely to fulfill our egalitarian goal of offering all people the opportunity to become self-confident and self-actualizing people. The more broadly we can define talent, the more opportunity we give people to be above-average. Statistically, it is possible for only 50 percent of the population to be above-average on a single dimension of talent. If, however, we value two unrelated kinds of ability, 75 percent of the people can be above-average on one or the other of the two dimensions. If we make room in society for recognizing three different talents, 87.5 percent can be above-average on at least one of the three abilities. Actually, of course, most abilities are correlated, but we can surely expand the opportunities for more people to be talented by expanding the dimensions of learning. Students and the society at large will benefit if the new egalitarian higher education can be redefined to mean high levels of performance rather than high levels of academic abstraction. The development of strong interpersonal skills, for example, may be a much more important objective for many new students and for society than the development of mediocre academic skills.

There has been much talk and some documentation of the increasing homogenization of higher education. The criticism has been that the community colleges were just aping the traditional models of the past. I have been among those critics, but Peterson's IGI data—admittedly from only one state—give me hope that the community colleges are beginning to carve out a distinctive mission for themselves.

They are expressing an interest in doing something much different from turning out mediocre academicians. Students, faculty, administrators, trustees, and the local citizenry of the community colleges show remarkably high agreement on the goals that they would like to see their colleges pursue. As a matter of fact, they show higher agreement on what their colleges should do than on what they are doing. The university community, on the other hand, agrees very well on what they are doing, but they show less unanimity when it comes to setting goals for the future. This finding seems to me to reflect the crisis in purpose for higher education. The traditional universities agree on what they are doing now, but they are struggling to reach agreement on what they should do in the changing world of higher education. In contrast, the new community colleges agree upon their future role in the new egalitarian education, but they need to gain experience and to reach agreement on the priorities of present programs.

The University of California constituencies, for example, agree wholeheartedly that their present emphasis is on research, advanced graduate and professional training, and on student acquisition of knowledge in the academic disciplines. They are not quite as united on what role the university should play in the new world of postsecondary education—except that the university should be an intellectually-oriented community. The community colleges, on the other hand, were established with certain ideals in mind about what they should accomplish. Thus people are reasonably clear about purpose. Three goals are invariably at the top of the list for all constituent groups of the community colleges. They are the vocational preparation of students, the creation of a community characterized by openness and trust, and attention to the personal development of students.

If the constituencies of the community colleges and the University of California are able to attain the high priority goals that those associated with each campus substantially agree upon, we would have two quite different institutional profiles that would be described something like this by the goal statements of the IGI:

(1) The community colleges would concentrate on helping students decide upon personal and vocational goals and would provide specific occupational training as well as opportunities for self-exploration and the development of self-confidence and interpersonal skills. Education would take place in an atmosphere of mutual trust and cooperation. Meeting the cultural, educational, and employment needs of the local community would also be an important objective.

(2) The University of California would concentrate on creating an intellectually stimulating environment in which faculty and students pursued scholarly inquiry and cultural activities in an atmosphere of mutual trust and cooperation. Students would be helped to develop a commitment to self-directed, life-long learning. The training of graduate and professional students would continue to receive important emphasis.

There are two diametrically opposed arguments regarding the value of community colleges in opening educational opportunity. One contends that the community colleges are not different enough from traditional institutions and that they therefore fail to serve their uniquely different clientele.[1] The other contends that they are too different and therefore likely to brand their students as different from, and inferior to, the graduates of traditional higher education.[2]

The latter argument would take us in the direction of greater homogenization of postsecondary education so that graduates would be indistinguishable one from another, in terms of credentials at least. The other position takes us in the direction of greater diversity and into the task of designing new and different educational experiences for different kinds of students. Advocates of each position accuse advocates of the other of wanting to resist change in traditional education—one by diverting "new students" into community colleges so that traditional institutions will not have to change, the other by assuming that all students can be served equally well by traditional education. There is no easy answer to this debate since the argument for open admissions to all institutions hinges largely on public attitudes: if the public thinks that a university education is better than a community college education, then, for many practical purposes such as employment, it is.

I suggest, however, that the business of educators is to educate. Students and society will be the losers in the long run if we permit education to be used as the instrument for certification rather than for its own purposes.

I believe that we should strive for maximum diversification in the education of the new world so that we can maximize our chances

[1] K. P. Cross, *Beyond the Open Door: New Students to Higher Education* (San Francisco: Jossey-Bass, 1971); and T. B. Corcoran, "The Coming Slums of Higher Education," *Change,* 1971, *4*(7), 30–35.

[2] J. Karabel, "Community Colleges and Social Stratification," *Harvard Educational Review,* 1972, *42*, 521–562.

of educating our diverse new clientele. Postsecondary education is too big and too influential now for us all to do the same thing at the same time. Earlier we all pursued the model of academic excellence, thus ignoring or relegating to secondary status the needs of educationally disadvantaged students. Today, the excitement and the action is in serving "new students" in higher education, but let us not make the error of ignoring the need to improve education for traditional and academically gifted college students. Diversity in institutions is needed to provide for the enormous variety present in our new clientele, but diversity in emphasis is also needed for national health and stability.

It is is, perhaps, too early to tell how smoothly we are making the transition to universal postsecondary education. We know that we have a long way to go before we can claim that there is a new world of postsecondary education for "new students."

11

The Seventies, Eighties, and Beyond

Hugh W. Lane

I must begin by informing the reader that this is not a finished essay. Its design calls for me to enumerate categories of persons excluded from higher education, to develop categories of higher educational institutions themselves, and from these to construct a grid, within each cell of which I would then make some remarks or observations about forces for change and forces for resistance to change within higher education. What I am attempting in these pages is to describe the grid and then to fill in only a few of the cells.

There are two other matters—these concern the use of certain terms—that should be mentioned before launching into the substance of this paper. First, in the remarks that follow, I use the term *white* racism advisedly and as an intentional public expression of my still considerable respect for Otto Kerner, the former Governor of the State of Illinois. Second, I use the term *higher education* in preference to *postsecondary education* in order to underline my personal view that the higher learning is entirely appropriate for new populations knocking at our doors. I fear that the use of the term *postsecondary education* may mean that many among us resist the growing presence of these emergent populations in our midst and wish they were somewhere else—in careers, in jobs, in the service, but not in higher education.

Everyone not white, Anglo-Saxon Protestant, and male has been a *victim* at one time or another during our history as a nation. In the course of our history, every person not a white Anglo-Saxon Protestant male has been excluded at some time and in some form. I wish to suggest that those excluded from higher education somehow fail to have the attributes of white Anglo-Saxon Protestant maleness.

The new population for higher education for the seventies and afterward will consist of those types presently comprising the college-attending group and those types presently excluded from college attendance by acts of omission or by acts of commission. These acts of omission or commission tend to favor white Anglo-Saxon Protestant males and to exclude those who are not white Anglo-Saxon Protestant males. I offer at least the following categories as suggestive of the various segments of our population presently neglected by or excluded from higher education.

(1) Those excluded by their inability to meet the costs of attendance.

(2) Those excluded by relative previous achievement as represented by school grades and scores on standardized achievement tests.

(3) Those excluded by imputed quality of previous schooling as viewed through imputed quality of the high school attended and the community or neighborhood served by the high school.

(4) Those excluded by scores on aptitude tests.

(5) Those excluded by race or ethnicity.

(6) Those excluded by language barriers.

(7) Those excluded as a result of the inadequacies of guidance, including tracking, as well as grossly inadequate ratios of counselors to students in most of our major urban school systems.

(8) Those excluded by gender. I allude both to the outright

exclusion of women and the none-too-subtle tracking of women toward careers seen as requiring training rather than education.

(9) Those excluded for previously rated low morality (crime, misbehavior, and so forth).

(10) Those excluded as risks to the institution.

(11) Those excluded for such things as late application, when seen as characteristic of group patterns.

(12) Those approaching college along nontraditional avenues: high school equivalency, alternate preparation, the work world, travel, and so forth.

(13) Those excluded by age—not only the older student, but also the even younger student.

Our present rationale for higher education asserts that it is for the more talented or the better prepared. Our planning for higher education assumes some sort of normative comparison which identifies the more "able" for inclusion and the less "able" for exclusion. Positive acts of inclusion or exclusion are accomplished through tracking, the testing mechanism, the guidance function, and the system of rewards and punishments.

Passive acts of inclusion or exclusion occur through: limited recruitment among groups whose characteristics differ from those of populations presently included; the interaction of various socio-psychological factors which sustain the correlation between test scores, achievement, and socio-economic status; differential perception of individual behaviors resulting from the fact that teachers, administrators, counselors, and other personnel of the schools are all products of the same cultural forces; differential reactivity to observed behaviors as a function of observed indicators of social class status; and caste-generated reactions by teachers and pupils.

These reactions by school personnel, students, and their parents are all the actions of individuals, but the behaviors assume the kind of regularity which indicates that they are lawful. Thus active intervention is required at the behavioral level if behavior modification is to result. And active intervention is called for. Behavior modification is called for. I call here not for modification in the behavior of the new student, but rather for modification in the behaviors of decision-makers such as counselors, teachers, administrators, admissions officers, financial aid officers, and faculty members. I call for modifications in education itself as an institutional form—as society's way of replicating itself while producing orderly change and growth. The new rationale for higher education must be based upon the joint assumptions of public good and public necessity. We can no longer be fearful of appearing so profound or so committed as to base our actions and procedures upon such high ground.

I am informed that among the black males of the college-attending age cohort for Washington, D.C., a higher number are fully on public support, in jail, or in prison than are in college in Washington, D.C. This is absurd economically and unbearable morally. Since few of us would argue that more time, more personnel, and more money should be devoted to penology and criminology than to socialization, training, and learning, can we consider turning our prisons into colleges? The budget is there. The numbers are there. The need is there. But higher education is not there, and our society is not there.

Models, role models, imitation, identification, oral incorporation of the ego ideal—these related concepts are germane to our discussion. The Coleman study of educational outcomes suggests most pointedly the peculiar efficacy of socioeconomically heterogeneous grouping in classes for producing achievement outcomes in students from lower SES groups. This may be a learning effect; it may be socialization. It may work both ways. That is, behaviors of students from lower SES groups may be taken over by students from higher SES groups. At any rate, there is considerable evidence from Coleman, from Stern and Pace, from Newcomb, and from others showing a sustained impact upon students and their ensuing life styles which would seem to be an effect of the composition of that grouping considered to be classmates or fellow students. Robert Berls summarized much of this evidence and conflicting evidence in one of his papers included in the compendium of papers submitted to the Joint Economic Committee of the 91st Congress. Suffice it to conclude that peers can have some effect upon each other.

What about other role models, other ego ideals? In a short essay entitled "The Immigrant," Eric Erikson noted that the child cannot achieve "identity" in a social order which will not or does not allow his grandfather to achieve "serenity." How much more meaningful does Elizabeth Johnson's postulate of the "parental figure surrogate" loom, given Erikson's forbidding surmise. If, indeed, this social order does not allow *our grandfathers* to achieve serenity, then what must we devise? We must of course press for black persons at all social levels and in all social positions, if for no other reason than to provide role models with which our children can identify without ego diffusion. It would of course be better if our grandfathers could achieve serenity.

I once made such a proposal to a major foundation. I asked for a million dollars a year to retire a selected number of my elders who were overage in grade but still in harness for pressing economic reasons, and in the way of the revolution. I argued that their minds and hearts were sound, their intellects intact, their instincts correct. I went so far as to argue that their basic problem was their ethnicity. Were they white, they would be paid heads of national commissions, paid board members, salaried consultants, foundation executives, vice presidents of national corporations. But our grandfathers are not white. They, too, are ipso facto victims of white racism.

They, even our honored elders, become our enemies. Epimethus and Prometheus, father and son, are ranged one against the other. Both, as *victims,* take up arms—one against the other—in a social order that does not allow our elders to achieve serenity or our children to achieve identity.

There are two separable lines of development as these new populations attain access to higher education. One is the development of new institutions; the second is the alteration of existing institutions as seen through changed admissions policies, revised hiring policies, quotas, curricula, special services, and the like.

The emergence of new institutions corresponds to the theory of the development of indigenous communities. The black community is merely one of those of which we speak. In regard to it, Brother Owusu Sadaukai has noted that it is a contradiction to go to white people and ask them to develop a black education program in the interest of black people. These emergent institutions will be black, red, brown, Appalachian, community, female, and so forth, representing the needs and aspirations of those communities previously neglected or excluded outright. Their emergence will point additionally to the need for new vehicles to accreditation, certification, and for legitimation, if they are to remain true to their original mission.

The pressures for funding and legitimacy, as if these new institutions are not, ipso facto, legitimate, will push them to become increasingly like existing institutions. Their existence will, to some extent, produce changes in existing institutions, but it will also take the pressure off existing institutions to change.

There is a progression almost akin to natural law by which

new institutions take on the character of older, established institutions and, in the process, move away from their original mission and constituency. This is to be guarded against—the storefront church becomes Riverside Church, the junior college becomes a university.

New institutions are, however, only a partial, and not necessarily the principal, response society will make to these emergent populations. Our present institutions will also increasingly admit these students and be changed by their presence. There will be considerable resistance within and without the academy to any such needed change. Vice President Agnew has become a spokesman against such change. Several Jewish organizations and some prominent Jewish faculty members seem to be against such change. They are particularly against affirmative action in hiring, in admissions, and in financial aid. Now, clearly, not all Jews take this position. For to stand athwart the aspirations of peoples is particularly un-Jewish.

I myself see their position as essentially defensive and protectionist. One indication emerges from the recent statement of Columbia University President William McGill, who estimated that about half its faculty is Jewish and not just coincidentally male. It is not to criticize Columbia University or higher education to say that something is awry if half the faculty of Columbia is Jewish male. Rather it is to criticize again native white American racism for these pockets of considerable Jewish talent and accomplishment which are so obviously needed at other action points in our society. Were it not for native white American racism, many of these Jews would be elsewhere. They would be in government and commerce, in foundations, and in law, representing our country at home and abroad, in banking and in trade, many would be presidents of major American universities and colleges. One would be the President of the United States, two would be cabinet members, several would be in the judiciary. I see this Jewish talent not so much *concentrated* in the faculty of Columbia as *restricted* to the faculty of Columbia. It is interesting to note that prominent in the vanguard of the women's liberation movement is the Jewish woman. One speculates as to what extent women's liberation is a reaction to a male Jehovah, a male rabbinate, and the archetypical patriarchal family.

It is high time for the educated Jewish male to join the vanguard of those actively fighting for full rights for all, including those of Jewish women and the excluded minorities, in all phases of our lives. For there is an enemy. We have seen his face, and we know his name. He is white male chauvinism and native American bigotry. He emerges from time to time as anti-black, anti-Mexican, anti-Indian, antipoor, antiwoman and anti-Semitic. His tactic is "divide and conquer." We must not be misled. We must not be divided, or we will surely be limited to the protection of those gains we think we have accomplished.

There are other ethnic concentrations resting upon considerable accomplishment. I watched several segments of the NCAA regional basketball tournament last spring with a sense of amazement. Had I not known, I would have thought the black colleges were playing each other. The coaches were white, the crowds were white, the players were—almost all, that is—black. Now I want black basketball players; I want black athletes. But as my prescient wife says: "They don't mind our running and jumping as long as we aren't reading, writing, and figuring." A WASP wag might paraphrase this remark in referring to the ethnic proportions at Columbia and say, "We don't mind them [the Jewish males] having Columbia, as long as they don't have the United States Treasury." We minorities expect higher education to produce minority theoretical nuclear physicists, political scientists, pharmacologists, and social workers—but we get basketball teams.

And yet I sympathize almost totally with those members of the Jewish Defense League, the spawn of Rabbi Meir-Kahane, who demanded that the New York Yankees and the New York Mets fill 24 percent of their rosters with Jewish ballplayers (New York City's Jewish population reportedly being 24 percent). I'm a bit older than they are—Marshall Goldberg was my hero, Saul Rogovin was my "Hamlet" of the mound, and I remember Sandy Koufax. At another time and another place I would tell them more about Wilmeth Sidat-Singh, the Hindu halfback, All-American at Syracuse, my landsman and kinsman; All-American and halfback, but not Hindu at all—but that's another story.

I have tried in these pages to suggest categories of persons presently excluded from higher education whose emergence at the gates and inside the walls will produce changes in higher education itself in the years ahead. New institutions emerge as one response to these excluded categories. Old institutional forms adapt or refuse to adapt to the presence of the formerly excluded. Change is called for, a change bringing our educational philosophies into closer conformity with the public policy of equality of access and opportunity. There is and will be resistance to these changes. Vested interests will be ranged against public policy, and arbiters of our fate will attempt to turn back to a public policy of exclusion. With perseverance and understanding and diligence, however, higher education will proceed in its new mission which is, and must be, education for all.

12

World Game: An Education in Education

Valentine Rossilli Winsey

When an infant begins to experience life, when he gurgles, coos and smiles, nobody tells him that he's engaging in communications. When he tries to turn over, to reach for a toy which is attached to his crib, nobody tells him that through scientific manipulation of his world, he's testing the laws of gravity and experimenting, therefore, in physics. In other words, the infant is born a comprehensive human being—a being whose curiosity, intuition, imagination and, above all, innate instinct to experiment, to probe, and to question ranges the gamut of human emotional, intellectual and physical capabilities.

However, as the child arrives at the most crucial point in his life, his first day of school, he is initiated straight away into the world of formal education. His natural curiosity to explore leads him, and in short order, to the perplexing realization that this innate drive of his for comprehensivity must be discarded. For instead of being encouraged to respond progressively to his own spontaneous questioning, he is presented with packages of learning derived from a "body of knowledge" designed around a single function—preparing him to make a living. The consequence is that his natural instinct to want to know about everything on the face of the earth, let alone inside himself, is dulled, continuously, to the point of extinction. Small wonder, then, that so many of our brightest students refuse to come to college. The pressure on them to have to know what to major in—— what to specialize in—keeps them away.

The time is long past due now for educators to recognize that the laws of nature are inviolable, and that human beings as creatures of nature can thrive best only on an educational bill-of-fare which is designed in accordance with those laws: laws that compel human innate capacity toward comprehensive learning.

This new educational bill-of-fare must be so redesigned as to overcome the mental, emotional, and physical anemia that has, from the very beginning, afflicted our educational system. It must make possible the training of human faculties for learning not just content, not just detail, but whole systems and their interrelationships.

Therefore, the time is ripe for educators to recognize that what students should be learning is an essential *minimum* amount of content (and whatever that may be has never been established), but a *maximum* amount of process. For learning is not just the acquisition of mere content, but the comprehension of where and how to ferret out facts, how to analyze them, and how to bring various disciplines together to focus upon whatever particular problem has to be solved. Seen in this way, learning need not be limited by time or in scope, but can continue throughout the life span.

Perhaps this sounds like a demand for a Renaissance Man in an age when that's impossible. But this is an age when it's more possible than ever before! A Renaissance man is someone who has a vast amount of knowledge at his command. The key words are *at his command,* not *stored in his brain.*

To store knowledge we've built countless libraries from which men can retrieve it. But, today, with knowledge and change accelerating at such astronomical rates as to pauperize the richest imagination, it is no longer possible for the largest library in the world, let alone the individual brain, to contain it all, and that is why we have created a new facility. It can not only store unprecedented amounts of information, but also make it instantaneously available. That new facility is the computer data bank.

Inasmuch as the implications of this new facility have had not the slightest effect on the educational system, we can conclude that, perhaps, educators have so overspecialized as to render themselves and the students obsolete. Consider that while the emergence of the computer data bank underscores the obsolescence of training for specialization, nevertheless, educators persist in myopic attempts to impart this ever-growing bulk of knowledge through relatively outmoded methods of teaching. Teaching in terms of one static entity, one so-called "body of knowledge," or one single problem.

Unfortunately, the first priority given to the computer data bank has been for the purpose of storing information that can be used primarily for solving the problem of how we can best destroy our enemies. All the hardware and software, all the information about psychological, natural and technological capabilities is now at the immediate command of top military leaders in the Pentagon. With the assistance of the Rand Corporation computers, all this information is being brought to bear on such problems as how we can best kill the Chinese, the Russians, or whomsoever we may decide must be killed.

What is more, this information is being continuously expanded and updated for the express purpose of "playing" the Von Neumann War Games. Ironically, this same information and more could be stored and applied to the solution of our universal human problems instead. And that is what comprehensive education is all about.

That is also what one of the most aggressive proponents of comprehensive education, R. Buckminster Fuller, is about. For more than a quarter of a century, he has been amassing an inventory of planet earth. Today, this inventory may constitute the most comprehensive compilation of information of just what resources our planet contains. For example, the location, rate of consumption, and regeneration of all of our physical resources are accounted for. The inventory answers such questions as: How much land and water does our planet contain? How much energy do we get from the winds, the oceans and the sun? What is the composition and effect of the one hundred thousand tons of stardust that falls on our planet daily? Fuller has also begun to collect information about our metaphysical resources, our concepts, our theories, inventions, and discoveries. Added to these will be the changing trends of human needs and of human behavior characteristics like birth and death rate patterns and political events, as well as the consequences of socio-economic developments.

Another vast body of information is being gathered by the United Nations. Still a third, and equally monumental, undertaking of similar purpose has been assumed by NASA. NASA's meteorological planet analysis and earth's resources satellites have cameras which take pictures that look as if they had been snapped one hundred feet from the ground. What is more, sensors on these satellites can pick up thermodynamic and electromagnetic frequencies with such accuracy as to make specific woods, furs, metals, and other materials recognizable by temperature. The numbers and whereabouts of cattle, and the location and size of industries and grain fields are just a few examples of all that can be accurately accounted for.

What must also be accounted for, however, is that this avalanche of ever-mounting informational content is continuously and predictably changing. This fact alone renders it all the more imperative that we shift our emphasis in the educational system from a focus on content to the study of process, instead—process attuned to the innate human capacity for comprehensive learning, and at the same time, attuned to preserve, exercise and, thereby, sharpen such additional priceless human attributes as intuition, imagination, the instinct to experiment, to compare and, above all, to continue to question.

One such process with extraordinary potential for training for comprehensive education has already been conceived by Fuller. He calls it "World Game." I had the privilege of participating in Fuller's World Game experiment when he launched it in 1969 in New York City. Since then, I've conducted several of my own, first on the undergraduate level at what was then known as Pace College and has since become Pace University. Later, I conducted it on the graduate level for the Special Programs Department of the United States Department of Agriculture's graduate school for government executives in Washington, D. C.

The first step in World Game is to get the participant to gather as many questions as possible regarding the problems on which he and his teammates would like to focus. This should lead to several important concomitant steps, but the primary goal is to revitalize the habit of questioning, and to skillfully lead the participant to the point of defining and redefining the problems. A most effective way is to get him to jockey back and forth between the information as it accumulates and the questions. Through this process each participant continues to gather as much information as he can about all that is presently known regarding our resources, be they human, natural or technological, which can be brought to bear on a chosen problem.

The second step is for him to join with the others in making his information available by rendering it visible. The participant does this by mounting and allocating his data on a large "playing board"— the dymaxion world map—thus contributing to the cumulative and graphic picture of where our resources are presently located, and how they are being distributed. (In the 1969 World Game experiment, for example, students discovered through their information and plotting of data that in 1967 Southeast Asia had imported as much rice as she had exported.) Such graphic representations on the dymaxion map also greatly facilitate, therefore, the task of identifying and circumscribing problems, as the students learn to look for trends. These trends begin to emerge when some of the data are extrapolated, and what is ultimately revealed is the manner and speed with which global resources are being used. Ultimately, the implications these trends may have for the future of humanity emerge with growing clarity and become the major focus of concern.

The students undertake the further step of correlating two or more trends, carefully assessing what is good and what is bad. Should a certain trend need to be augmented or altered, everyone joins in the effort to design possible solutions. No solution, however, is accepted at face value. It is extensively tested for its viability by being subjected to rigorous questioning: Have we taken into account all of the possible known variables that bear on our problem? Does our simulated design accomplish its purpose without negative effects on our environment? Does the solution interfere in the slightest with the well-being of others anywhere on the globe? Does it help us to achieve more with less?

Here is a concrete example of a game. One of my Pace students investigated worldwide literacy. While she was gathering and mounting the data on the percentages of literacy in various areas throughout the world, another student happened to be investigating global paper consumpion and, of course, the resulting use of forest land. In studying the dymaxion map, the first student was struck by two correlations. One showed that the higher the literacy of a country, the greater its use of paper; the other revealed that as literacy throughout the world went up, there was a concomitant increase in the use of paper, and of the available softwood trees with which to make the paper. More questions were generated as students grappled with the problem of how to create a greater percentage of world literacy. The inquiry involved them in further investigation of the supply of softwood and various possible methods for creating synthetic paper.

Another example may be cited from the first World Game group of 1969 in which I participated. At issue was the question of electrical energy supply. It was discovered that we in the United States are gobbling it up at an unprecedented rate. So much so, that we are threatened with continuous brownouts and blackouts, whereas, in many parts of the world there is no electrical power available at all. The threat for people in those areas is an ever-greater exacerbation of their present problems, including starvation, inadequate housing, swelling population, and so on. In short, lack of that most essential life-sustaining resource, electrical energy, means that civilization, rather than merely standing still, may well be going backward.

We pondered the possibility of doubling the electrical output of all power plants presently in existence, so as to make it amply available not only for ourselves, but for everyone in the world. It was a naive enough supposition at first glance, yet, this was the very starting point we chose. Our additional research revealed some startling facts. First, that our latest technological development had brought us to a point where we could now transmit extremely high voltage, and without the slightest loss, over a span of fifteen hundred miles. That is almost double the feasible distance of yesterday's technology.

A second startling fact revealed that all power plants are maximally productive only during the day. Those periods when power is reduced because of reduced needs at night, however, meant that the maximal efficiency of each plant was not being utilized. We wondered why such waste is allowed. Why not keep all power plants operating at maximum efficiency day and night and build new ones wherever needed for a possible relay system on a global scale? Wouldn't such a strategy make it possible for all people to plug into this life-sustaining resource? Wouldn't such a scheme lead to the realization of a planetary grid—a circulatory energy system comparable to our own blood system? We explored all possible pros and cons, including such considerations as the additional need for copper for building new power lines, additional materials for buildings and equipment, the additional fuels that would be necessary, and so on. Our conclusion was that not only was all this feasible, but that, indeed, it would enable us to do more with less, and for the benefit of all humanity.

This proposal for a global electrical energy grid was presented by the former chairman of the Atomic Energy Commission, Glen Seaborg, to the United Nations, where it is under consideration. It is characteristic of the kind of solution that would have been impossible to devise, had one approached the problem of energy resource from the point of view of just one or two disciplines.

What I have described are two examples of the kinds of discoveries that are possible with an educational tool like "World Game." Those who participated in the various experiments received a very liberal dose of comprehensive education. They learned that it was not important, let alone possible, to know practically everything about one discipline. They learned that what is important is to be able to see the information from various disciplines and to approach a problem comprehensively. They could see, for instance, what trends were causing a problem to exist, and what other trends the existence of a problem was causing. This in turn enabled them to speculate on new correlations—through the application of intuition and imagination—in order to arrive at solutions to problems which take into account as many of the variables and side effects as could be found.

And in the process, students came to realize not only the enormous variety of information that is available to them, but also the extraordinary rapidity with which so much of that information keeps changing. The potential of such insight for inducing them to examine further their own basic assumptions about themselves, humanity, their world, and other vital concepts can hardly be assessed.

13

Limits to Growth

Dennis L. Meadows, Lewis Perelman

Each of us, whether a professor or an administrator in higher education, is responsible in some way for structuring an educational environment within which students can acquire skills, personal values, perceptual habits, and a knowledge of facts and theories. Those acquisitions will determine in large measure the extent to which our current students are able to pursue fruitful careers over the next fifty years. In the year 2000 today's students will be only half way through their professional careers. Thirty years from now, what assessment will they make of the education we provided them today? What personal, organizational, and national problems will they have had to understand and help resolve? What knowledge, what concepts of justice, of self, and of social goals will prove ultimately to have been the best basis for our student's contribution to the orderly evolution of this social system?

Our educational efforts are based on two important concepts. The first is a concept of the necessary content of education; it is derived from an image of the resources, the constraints, the values, and the personal goals that are likely to characterize this society in the coming decades. The second is a concept of the ethical foundations of formal educational processes, that is, the rights and obligations implicit in each student-teacher relationship.

Until quite recently in the history of mankind, the rate of material and demographic change was very slow. Technology, the level of population, and economic activity did not increase radically during the lifetimes of most individuals. One could thus identify through the study of history most of the important attributes of future society. The traditional goals of education and the nature of academic ethics could be modified gradually on the basis of experience. Now, however, the culmination of numerous global trends virtually ensures that our students will have to face a spectrum of challenges unprecedented in history. We must now complement the study of the past with an explicit examination of the future. From that analysis will come an improved basis for determining the most appropriate goals and premises of current education.

During the past two years a group of scientists and students have worked at MIT in a systematic effort to understand the causes and the future consequences of growth in the world's population and material output, two factors that will have a dominant influence on the global society within which our students will live. Their conclusions were presented in a non-technical summary, *The Limits to Growth:*[1]

(1) If the present growth trends in world population, industrialization, pollution, food production, and resource depletion continue unchanged, the limits to growth on this planet will be reached sometime within the next one hundred years. The most probable result will be a rather sudden and uncontrolled decline in both population and industrial activity.

(2) It is possible to alter these growth trends and to establish a condition of ecological and economic stability that is sustainable far into the future. The state of global equilibrium could be designed so that the basic material needs of each person on earth are satisfied and each person has an equal opportunity to realize his individual human potential.

(3) If the world's people decide to strive for this second out-

---

[1] D. H. Meadows and others, *The Limits to Growth* (New York: Universe Books, 1972).

come rather than the first, the sooner they begin working to attain it, the greater will be their chances of success.

The analysis that led to these results was conducted through the construction and the simulation of computer models of important global relationships. While computer modeling is an efficient way to summarize and analyze large amounts of data, the underlying premises of the study can be readily described and understood without recourse to computers. It is the premises of the research, not the detailed computer charts presented in *Limits to Growth,* that form the basis for this discussion. The global decline portrayed in *Limits* is not inevitable. It only appears to be the most likely outcome of current trends. If educators can understand the foundations of the study and respond constructively to the challenges they pose, those trends can be altered. The purpose of this presentation is to summarize the basic assumptions underlying the study of limits to growth and to describe several of their implications for the process of higher education.

Five attributes of the global system lead to the conclusions set forth in *Limits to Growth.* There will be no attempt here to "prove" the validity of all five assertions, since these five aspects of global society are obvious to most individuals. They have, in any event, been fully described elsewhere.[2] It will be useful here only to describe each aspect quickly and to illustrate its global aspects.

First, most material and demographic aspects of the global system are growing at a rate unprecedented in history. Until very recently in man's tenure on earth his population and economic activities grew globally at rates that caused them to double over periods of one thousand to two thousand years or more. Now population is increasing at a rate that will cause it to double within about thirty years, and the rate of global population growth is increasing. Resource consumption and the release of pollutants are both growing at rates that will cause them to double within the next ten to twenty years.

Second, there are many inescapable physical limits to material growth. The capacity of the environment to absorb material or thermal emissions, the ability of the land to produce food, and the ability of the earth to yield economically useful deposits of nonrenewable resources are all finite. Technology cannot eliminate these limits, it can only permit society to use the resources of the earth somewhat more

---

[2] Meadows and others, *Limits to Growth;* D. L. Meadows and D. H. Meadows (Eds.), *Toward Global Equilibrium; Collected Papers* (Cambridge, Mass.: Wright-Allen Press, 1973).

efficiently. These and other limits indicate that material and demographic growth will ultimately cease. For reasons cited in *Limits to Growth*, we may expect that the transition from growth to equilibrium will be substantially completed during the lifetimes of our students.

The third fact has been aptly expressed by Commoner: "Everything is connected to everything else."[3] No important part of the global society is completely disconnected from the others. For example, U.S. energy policy in the future will influence the amount of dollars available to Middle Eastern countries for the pursuit of their own political objectives. The policy will alter the price of oil imported into India, and it will affect the global climate, the U.S. environment, and the relative affluence and political power of several major U.S. industries. The energy problem is not a technical problem alone. It involves aspects of the world normally sequestered within the disciplines of political science, economics, geology, business administration, regional planning and other fields. The solution of problems in transportation, in food production, in environmental protection, and in housing will similarly affect may other aspects of global society.

The fourth attribute of the global society is the long time delay inherent in cause and effect relationships, whether physical, biological, social, political, economic, or other. For example, once U.S. birth rates drop to replacement levels, the population of our country will still grow for seventy years because of the momentum inherent in the age distribution of the population. Even after we begin to decrease the rate of DDT usage, the level of DDT in the marine environment will still continue to rise for 20 years or more. There will still be DDT present in marine fish in significant amounts well beyond the year 2020. Having now perceived the crisis engendered by the impending depletion of its domestic fossil fuel deposits, it may take the U.S. five years to determine its long-term goals for energy use, ten years more to develop the appropriate technologies, and ten to twenty years more, at a minimum, to implement those new technical capabilities so that they begin to have a significant effect on the production and consumption of energy. Social relationships may involve the greatest delays of all. For example, the U.S. has been working for more than a hundred years to eliminate racial discrimination, and the job has not yet been accomplished.

[3] Barry Commoner, *The Closing Circle* (New York: Bantam Books, 1972), p. 29.

The fifth fact is that virtually all of our economic and political actions are based on an assessment only of near-term consequences. Those in politics care little for the benefits or the costs of their actions that will become apparent after the next election. Industrialists use a high rate of interest to determine the present monetary equivalent of the future costs and benefits of current alternatives. With the interest rates commonly used, 10 to 15 percent, no consequence of an act further than five or ten years into the future is of any economic interest to industrialists today. Even individuals are short sighted. All of us allocate our creative energies to the problem with the closest deadline, not to issues with the most important long-term consequences.

The three conclusions of *Limits to Growth* cited above are simply a logical consequence of these five facts. Any system will be unstable if it grows rapidly, has limits, is highly interrelated, incorporates long delays, and is governed by short-term perspectives. All of man's social, technological, economic, and political institutions are thus inherently unstable—that is, they have a tendency to overshoot their long-term goals. There are many illustrations of this fact. It is clear that the global population has already overshot the levels which would permit satisfaction of the goals of health, education and economic opportunity for all. The U.S. Commission on Population Growth and the American Future could find no economic or social advantage in an increased population. Consider then by how much the populations of less industrialized areas have grown past their most desirable levels. Today in the U.S. it is clear that the energy system has also overshot the current limits to its ability to produce inexpensive and environmentally acceptable energy. The *Limits to Growth* results are simply global extrapolations of events that are already clear in more restricted areas.

Those who accept the above conclusions should immediately accept six challenges to the content, processes, and goals of traditional education: make the content problem-oriented; broaden the concept of education to include more than learning how to store and retrieve verbal information; dispense with the concept of disciplines; recognize that education may be the displacement rather than merely the acquisition of knowledge; provide an ecological conscience; and present a new concept of man along with the tools and facts that are taught. The remainder of this presentation discusses these challenges and the ways in which they may be met.

Today, higher education is predominantly structured around

disciplines instead of real world problems. We teach our students a set of facts and theories that are grouped together only because they are derived by making the same simplifying assumptions about the real world or because they were developed through use of the same analytical procedures. Unfortunately, the real world is not neatly divided into disciplines. We would laugh at a geographer who chose to specialize in only the areas that lay between two adjacent topographic lines on his maps, say between eight hundred and nine hundred feet above sea level. Topographic lines are, of course, an artifact derived solely from our units of measurement. They do not exist in the real world. As a consequence, students of the geographer would not be able to navigate in the real world on the basis of what they had learned in his courses.

Unfortunately the divisions between the traditional disciplines, for example economics and politics, are as artificial and unrelated to real world processes as the topographic lines on a map. The material taught in any one discipline is not alone sufficient for solving *any* significant social problem. Thus, we must complement the traditional disciplines with programs structured around real world problems. These new programs will take their content not from the stages of historical development of a disciplinary field but from the phases of real world problem solving: problem identification, data gathering, analysis, design of alternative solutions, choice from among competing alternatives, implementation, and assessment. Specifically we must shift the content of education to accomplish the following things:

(1) Imbue our students with the recognition that the future can be deliberately created. It need not be just passively experienced. (2) Provide students with an intuitive appreciation for the causes and the consequences, the costs and the benefits of material growth and social change. (3) Provide formal, methodological tools for making useful statements about the future consequences of current actions. (4) Teach how complex systems change over time. The social sciences deal primarily with static systems at equilibrium. The important real world problems are associated with physical and social systems that are always in disequilibrium. (5) Convey the notion of uncertainty, and teach the best use of partial information. (6) Provide skills in the design of experiments to gather more information and teach techniques for analyzing data in order to identify causal relationships. (7) Introduce the time dimension explicitly. Current actions have long-term consequences. Students should be trained to understand those distant

results. They should be given the ethical foundation required when contemplating an action that is beneficial in the short run but whose costs must be borne by others. (8) Acknowledge explicitly that man is destined to live in a finite world that will always impose some constraints on the range of options. The image of a future utopia must be replaced with a vision of a limited world filled with difficult trade-offs. Students should learn to make choices which inevitably involve compromise. (9) Describe the behavior of real world organizations. Without a realistic understanding of the motivations and the leverage points in industrial and political bureaucracies, our students will inescapably be frustrated at their inability to bring desirable changes in the organizations that govern so much of modern life. (10) Teach the concept that goals adapt slowly over time in response to new information.

In short we must decrease the emphasis on teaching facts and theories, most of which will be incorrect or irrelevant within a few years. Instead we should change the content of higher education so that it provides our students with skills necessary to identify their own theories and to assess the accuracy and the relevance of those theories in a milieu of consantly expanding knowledge and changing goals.

While the changes outlined above are necessary, they are not sufficient. To meet the challenges posed by the limits to growth we must also alter our concept of the ethics underlying formal education. The predominant conception of what the process of education is and ought to be is so narrow that it will be difficult to extend the content of education in the directions indicated above. Many educators harbor the rather naive belief that if only the *facts* about the ecological and social crises confronting man could be widely disseminated then the majority of men, being rational, would join in pursuit of the goal of global equilibrium. Yet no one is predominantly rational in his behavior. A vast educational campaign has been underway for some years now to make people aware of the facts linking cigarette smoking with disease and death; there is probably not a smoker in America who does not know that smoking is likely to impair his health and decrease his life expectancy, and yet cigarette sales climb higher and higher. Thus "education" has not even made people act in their own long-term self interest.

What is required is nothing less than for educational processes to become part of a social servo-mechanism which can gain control of a world run amok and which can lead it toward, and maintain it in, a state of sustainable equilibrium. Such a mechanism must be capable of cultivating the kinds of human knowledge, attitudes, and behaviors that are commensurate with a state of global equilibrium, and therefore must embrace the full range of non-coercive behavior control technology. What such a mechanism should be called—whether education, communication, persuasion, propaganda—is somewhat immaterial as long as the essential function is recognized. We prefer the term *ecological education*. *Ecological* because the goal is to resolve a situation of global ecological crisis by the establishment and maintenance of global, ecological equilibrium. *Education* because, in spite of the often narrowly-restricted connotations of the word, it derives from the Latin verb *educare,* which means "to lead forth," precisely what a mechanism for moving our society towards the stationary state must do.

Ecological education, then, must be an effective mechanism for producing individual and social changes on a global basis to steer human society away from its current collision course with ecological catastrophe. It must be clearly understood, moreover, that when we speak of ecological education we are not merely discussing some esoteric subset of the general educational system, like adult education, or sex education, but rather are speaking of a new vision of the meaning of education in terms of both goals and processes.

First, we must open up our conception of the processes of education to embrace all phenomena that influence the cybernetic process called learning. The fundamental weakness of our traditional conception of education is that it is based on an erroneous model of learning. For this reason, Illich finds *schooling* to be not only irrelevant, but even antithetical to true learning. Pre-ecological education envisions learning as an essentially linear, open-ended process: information deemed relevant by the "educational system" is transmitted from the teacher to the student where it is to be processed and stored and later retrieved for the purpose of testing to see whether the information has been processed correctly and is still in storage.

True learning is a nonlinear, closed-ended, looped or cyclical process. In its simplest conception, learning requires identification of the *gestalt* of organism-in-environment—a capacity for the organism, or individual, to interact or respond to its environment, and *feedback* to the organism from its interaction or response. Feedback is what makes learning a cyclical process, a closed loop. Without feedback, communication between an individual and his environment can result in the exchange of information, but not in learning.

But feedback is only a necessary, and not a sufficient, condition for learning to take place. Communication between individual and environment and feedback on the individual's response to the environment only insure that it is possible for the individual to exercise some degree of *control* over his relationship with the environment. Learning enables one not merely to control his behavior within a given environment, but further to *adapt* to novel or changing conditions in the environment. Such adaptation implies a process of induction, or generalization over past interactions with the environment according to some criterion.

In simple terms, learning always requires the process of *experimentation*, of trial-and-error. It is clear where the antithesis between schooling and learning lies; learning requires trials and errors, but schooling frustrates trials and punishes errors. This is not to say that learning does not take place within the system of schooling; but the learning which does occur is largely incidental and those who do learn are merely monitored, graded, and classified by the system, and then at the end of the schooling process are channeled into various social and economic strata, according to the amount of information they have processed. The schooling system does very little to cultivate learning and a great deal to stifle it by its overwhelming insistence on information-processing as the fundamental model of system performance.

But if the schooling system has been hostile, or even just indifferent, to this initial, or *proto* level of learning, there is yet a higher level of learning—what Gregory Bateson has labelled *deutero-learning*. Deutero-learning is the process of "learning how to learn." (This requires feedback of a still higher order, or different logical type, than simple or *proto-learning*.) Schooling assigns value to students according to their capacity for learning with the minimal number of trials and errors; it is not surprising then that IQ, which measures this capacity, is a strong predictor of academic success. But there is nothing sacrosanct or especially valuable about this particular style of learning, except that it interferes minimally with the information-processing activity with which the schooling system fills most of its time, and that it also interferes minimally with the socioeconomic stratification process which the system serves so well. In any case, whether out of malice or indifference or sheer blindness, the schooling system does nothing to cultivate deutero-learning, the learning of the skills of learning itself.

It is at the level of deutero-learning, as well as at the level of proto-learning, that the major work of ecological education needs to be done. Simply imparting information about the ecological crisis will do little to effect the kinds of changes in human behavior that are necessary for planetary survival. Even if we succeed in cultivating the kind of learning necessary to enable people to adapt themselves to the new conditions of a state of global equilibrium, we will not have gone far enough. Ultimately, we are going to have to cultivate a new, ecological consciousness, initially among those who exercise the greatest degree of control over the dynamics of the social-ecological system and eventually among the population as a whole. We must teach people new modes of thinking and of knowing, and this necessarily means learning new ways of learning. Thus ecological education must function at the level of deutero-learning, and perhaps even beyond.

Perhaps one of the best descriptions of a holistic, ecological mode of thinking is provided by Robert Heinlein's contemporary classic science-fiction novel, *Stranger in a Strange Land*.[4] Valentine Michael Smith, the hero, is a human whose singular fate was to be raised from infancy by Martians. Smith's body may be human, but his mind is distinctly Martian, vastly exceeding in power even the most extraordinary terrestrial mind. The initial and most important lesson that he teaches his human comrades is the art of *grokking*. *Grok* is a Martian word that can only be understood—or grokked—by induction, that is, by reading the book. Essentially, however, the word means to comprehend something completely, holistically, in all its fullness, with the additional connotation of loving, cherishing and praising.

The grokking mode of thought seems to be emerging as a major fallout of modern computer technology, especially in the fields of systems analysis in general and in Jay Forrester's system dynamics methodology in particular. One finds more and more people in these fields talking about "thinking in systems," in a manner strongly reminiscent of Heinlein's grokking. Jay Forrester has observed that complex systems—systems characterized by high-order, nonlinear, multiloop feedback structure—are predominantly "counterintuitive" in their behavior. Therefore they are best analyzed and understood with the help of

[4] Robert A. Heinlein, *Stranger in a Strange Land* (New York: Berkeley Medallion Books, 1968).

formal models and high-speed computers. But many of Forrester's colleagues and students have found that experience with system dynamics eventually enables them to *grok* the behavior of complex systems to a large extent without the machine's assistance; hence the rise of "thinking in systems."

The relevance of all this to the ecological crisis is apparent to anyone familiar with the science of ecology. The laws of nature are not independent of each other; living things are not autonomous. Neither the laws nor the things they govern can be understood as discrete entities, since they are all ravelled in an elaborate knot called the ecosystem. Forrester's caveat regarding the counterintuitive behavior of complex systems has its analog in Barry Commoner's aphoristic fourth law of ecology: "There's no such thing as a free lunch."[5] Biologist Garrett Hardin says the same thing a little differently: We can never do merely one thing. To comprehend the ecosystem it is not enough to merely know the parts of it; rather one must be able to *grok* the whole.

Ecological consciousness then is the grokking-level awareness of the global ecosystem, of its synergetic behavior, of its complexity, of its connectedness, and of the place and role of man within its multidimensional web. Since the global ecosystem includes all biomes and biocenoses as well as all anthropocentrically-defined "man-made" (as if distinct from "natural") systems—such as cities, corporations, governments, railroads, schools—as subsystems, ecological consciousness is a holistic vision of on-going, worldwide life processes in synergetic combination. In cultivating ecological consciousness, the emphasis must be on process and form, on cybernetic structure, on unifying principles that govern dynamic behavior, rather than on categorical pigeon-holing, naming of parts, simplistic pairing of cause and effect. To put it metaphorically, the emphasis must be on the rules of the game and the strategy of the play, rather than on the score of the game and the names of the players.

Holistic education in "systems thinking" can only be accomplished by extracting education from the narrow mindedness of disciplines and departments. The response to the urgent need for ecological education by educational professionals has, to a discouraging extent, been parochial at best and self-serving at worst. Not only has the response to date been grossly inadequate in total scope, but what work has been done in this field has been seriously vitiated by a double-

---

[5] Commoner, *Closing the Circle,* p. 41.

barreled parochialism: a parochialism of form, and a parochialism of content.

The parochialism of form derives from professional specialization in educational media: in-school, out-of-school, mass media, and so forth. Those working in the established school system often discount or disparage out-of-school or nonformal approaches. Those specializing in the latter may sympathize with Illich's deprecation of schooling and disdain any effort carried on within the educational establishment. Those who consider themselves communication specialists regularly eschew any identification with the field of education, and sometimes look down their noses at any educator who has the temerity to venture onto their elite turf.

The parochialism of content has perhaps an even more debilitating effect on efforts to promulgate an ecological consciousness. This parochialism is characterized by the fragmentation of the content of what should be ecological education into almost countless subsets. At the highest level, there is the schism between population education on the one hand, and environmental education on the other. Beyond this chimerical dichotomy there are even more subdivisions. On the population side we have demographic education, family planning education, sex education, family life education, and so on. On the environment side we have ecology education, conservation education, health education, urban studies, forestry, environmental law, and so on.

These two kinds of parochialism, of content and form, hobble our efforts to develop a truly ecological pedagogy, an educational process which is ecological not only in subject matter, but in its structure and dynamics as well. The content of ecological education must be as broad as the content of human life itself. It must be directed at all four dimensions of human development: intellectual, emotional, physical, and spiritual. Furthermore it must operate through all of the media that comprise the total learning environment. This means we must broaden our concept not only of what is education, but even more importantly, of who is an educator. The ranks of educators include more than just school teachers and college professors, they include journalists, politicians, lawyers, clergymen, union leaders, advertising executives, physicians, corporation presidents, and others. In short, an educator is anyone who cultivates learning in others. It is crucially important that we understand who the educators in our society are, because the first objective of ecological education must be to educate the educators, to cultivate their ecological consciousness so that they may integrate it into their roles and goals within the society.

In the Heavenly City of St. Augustine, evil was viewed as a negative or neutral force, in the sense that evil was only the absence of good or the lack of virtue. Thus the way to eliminate evil or sin was to augment or proliferate good or virtue. On the other hand, the Manichean vision found evil to be a positive force which actively and deviously combatted the forces of good and virtue.

In the ecological context, many educators have worked on the tacit assumption that the anti-ecological consciousness is an Augustinian, passive kind of evil, not so much an active antagonist as a pervasive ignorance, a lack of awareness which can be overcome by the dissemination of information, and rational discussion. This is not to say that the environmental movement as a whole has not been characterized by a Manichean viewpoint, because of course it often has. The rhetoric of environmentalism has been replete with bad guys, from robber barons to radical liberals; but the educators have generally envisioned themselves, quite ingenuously, as standing above, and being insulated from, these dialectics, on a pinnacle of scholarly objectivity. The result of this Augustinian view of the ecological crisis in the field of education is that many educators active in this area have emphasized *expansion* of learning rather than *displacement*. That is, since they view the anti-ecological conscience, or ecological ignorance, as being neither willful nor malicious, the efforts of these educators tend to stress increasing awareness of various aspects of the ecological crisis, with the naive expectation that their efforts will result in the salubrious alteration of the basic human attitudes and behaviors that lie at the very heart of the crisis itself. Since they do not recognize, or at least do not admit the existence of, any countervailing, anti-educating force save passive ignorance, they generally deprecate any educational process that can be stigmatized as persuasion, indoctrination, or propaganda.

But the fact is that the alternative to ecological education is not merely the vacuum of ignorance. In reality, our society is largely shaped and governed by an elaborate and potent system of anti-ecological education that permeates the total learning environment (the school, the home, the peer group, the media), as well as the physical environment itself. The system teaches us from the cradle to the grave all of the cardinal lessons that underlie the very internecine situation in which we now find ourselves: make babies, build, buy, consume, waste, fight wars, dump, burn, hate, escape, obey, make more babies, buy more things, make more money, get a higher position, get a bigger house, drive a bigger car, more is better, bigger is superior, growth is wonderful, everybody wins. This is the litany of what Herman Daly calls "Growthmania," and it pervades and reverberates through every corner of our society; it bombards us from every direction and via all the communication-education media that constitute the total learning environment. In fact, since McLuhan tells us that the medium *is* the message, it is clear that these media not only deliver the message of dysecology, but also are, in and of themselves, dysecological.

So the ecological educator, to be truly effective, must adopt a Manichean view of the challenge which confronts him. It is not enough to spread the gospel of ecology, one must also attack the devil. Satan, in this case, is the system of anti-ecological education, a powerful force at loose in the world today that is actively working to widen the gap between fertility and mortality, and to promote irresponsible parenthood. A force that is huckstering the meretricious dream of material affluence, and fueling the fires of economic imperialism and ecological devastation. The people of the world are not going to stop their headlong rush to disaster unless someone persuades them to do so. The magnitude of the task is awesome. We must convince the leaders, the educators of the world—the statesmen, politicians, businessmen, planners, journalists, teachers, soldiers, preachers—to radically alter not only their most basic policies and beliefs, but their total behavior and lifestyles, in fact, their total consciousness.

The fifth challenge lies in creating a new ethical basis for action. There are certain broad principles and rules of conduct which are assumed to shape, if not actually control, the behavior of any society. Written or unwritten, values, ethics, or morals are fairly ubiquitous notions of what a society ought to do, if not what it actually does. Taken in toto, these things comprise what we commonly call conscience.

The dividing line between conscience and consciousness is necessarily vague. Regardless of one's philosophy, it is evident that the viability of any system of ethics, of any social conscience, must be grounded upon the conception of reality as reflected in consciousness. Thus men who owned slaves could write that "all men are created equal, endowed by their Creator with certain inalienable rights;" this posed no moral dilemma for those whose consciousness classified slaves as property and not as men. Conscience constitutes a set of guidelines for behavior, but a set of guidelines that is only applied in certain circumstances that are defined by a model of reality, that is, by consciousness. Distortions and loopholes in our consciousness therefore create morally neutral territory in the real world, moral free-fire zones where individual and collective human behavior are freed from any ethical constraint, and are governed solely by the dictates of expediency.

It is no surprise that the road to hell is paved with good intentions. Conscience, uninformed by the apt perception of reality provided by a valid consciousness, creates its own devils. Mankind's highest moral principles have provided the strongest motivation for history's greatest abominations. And the trend is still going strong, as events in Vietnam, in Northern Ireland, in Bangladesh, and in the so-called Holy Land have demonstrated so graphically. So it is equally unsurprising that our frenetic social crises are embedded within a more vast, more virulent, and unattenuated ecological crisis. At a time when we should be learning to treat animals and other living things like men, humanely, we are still treating men like animals.

The ecological conscience then is not far different from our established collection of moral-ethical guides to human behavior. The major difference is that the ecological conscience enlarges the relevant universe of established moral-ethical principles to embrace the entire ecosystem. It is not necessary therefore to found a completely new, ecological religion in order to promulgate the ecological conscience. It would be enough if our existing theology or philosophy could adapt to a more viable model of reality—to a new ecological consciousness. This will only come as we combine better knowledge of the physical environment with a more subtle understanding of man.

It has long been a popular view among environmentalists that the ultimate roots of our ecological crisis lie in our fundamental consciousness. However this recognition often breaks down into a dialectic between Western and Eastern modes of thought. The former are given most of the blame for our current predicament, and the latter are advanced as the keys to salvation. Lynn White, Jr., originally put forth the thesis that the historical roots of our ecological crisis derive from the most basic tenets of the Western, Judeo-Christian tradition, citing, for example, the Biblical mandate for man to have "dominion over the earth." White's thesis has been absorbed into the thinking of many leading figures in the environmental field, such as Ian McHarg, who asserts that the essential source of our current ecological plight is "the very core of our tradition, the Judeo-Christian-Humanist view which is so unknowing of nature and of man, which has bred and sustained his simple-minded anthropocentrism and anthropomorphism."[6] Thus many have been led to embrace those oriental disciplines which seem most alien to occidental thought—Zen, The Tao, Vedanta and Yoga—as *the* ecological mode of thinking.

This view of Western thought as anti-ecological, and Eastern thought as ecological, has some objective basis, yet ultimately it is too simplistic to be very useful. It is true that many of the root causes of our ecological crisis can be traced to dysfunctional aspects of Western thought, but many of those aspects can also be found in traditions other than the Judeo-Christian one. In fact, our current ecological crisis is not the first one in human history; man has precipitated ecological crises throughout his history and on every continent. Civilization of any kind, East or West, being necessarily based on agriculture, has always resulted in severe, and often fatal, stress. Only tribal peoples, living predominantly as hunter-gatherers, have managed to remain largely in harmony with the natural environment.

The Western mode of thought admittedly has many dysecological aspects to it. As McHarg says, it is anthropocentric and anthropomorphic, setting man apart from, and dominant over, nature, viewing man as Godlike, or, perhaps more significantly, God as manlike. The emphasis on materialism, on hierarchy, on the conquest of nature, on the Protestant ethic, all have had their ecologically deleterious side-effects. But there are positive aspects as well. There is a strong underlying altruism. There is the emphasis on science and art, a respect for reason and natural law, an impulse toward intellectual advancement. It is significant that the old conservation and the more recent environmental movements are distinctly Western phenomena.

Of course the Eastern mode of thinking has much to recommend it, both generally and particularly, from an ecological point of view. Where the Western mode of thinking is anthropocentric, linear, discrete, and simplistic, the Eastern mode is cosmic, nonlinear, continuous, and complex, which makes it far more congruent with ecological reality. But the Eastern mode also tends to fatalism, passivity, anti-technicalism and anti-intellectualism, which are not very helpful attributes for dealing with the kinds of pressing problems that make up today's ecological crisis.

We need to work toward a mode of thinking that combines

---

[6] Ian L. McHarg, *Design with Nature* (New York: Doubleday–Natural History Press, 1971).

desirable aspects of both Eastern and Western as well as other, more "primitive," modes of thinking, in order to develop human minds that are better suited to comprehending the truest and most vital nature of reality. This last is our greatest challenge.

The economist John Stuart Mill was able in 1857 to foresee the ultimate end to rapid material growth. His questions in response to that perception posed a challenge that has been ignored for over a century: "Towards what ultimate point is society tending by its industrial progress? When the progress ceases, in what condition are we to expect that it will leave mankind?"

The answers to his questions are not yet given. While the transition to material equilibrium is inevitable, the path is not. However it comes about, our students' actions will now largely influence the nature of the steady state that lies ahead. If we as educators ignore the challenges, our students will have little perception or control over the forces that stop growth. Equilibrium will be imposed through natural and social processes outside their control. The collapses of civilizations past suggest that the process would be likely to serve no one's objectives. If we can acknowledge and respond constructively to the challenges posed by limits to growth then I believe we can provide the intellectual and moral foundation for a stable and just equilibrium that provides well for man's basic needs.

PART FOUR

Transcending
Role-Play

"There is nothing inherent in the genes of a working class kid that makes him more suited to fixing cars, and in those of a Boston Brahmin that makes him more adept at repairing limbs," we are told by Alison R. Bernstein in the essay (Chapter Fourteen) that opens Part Four. But educational institutions persist in casting our students in such socially determined roles. And as Edward Joseph Shoben, Jr., tells us in the last essay of this section (Chapter Eighteen), the academic standards by which "success" is judged aid and abet the psychology of role-play. All members of the American academic community—students, professors, trustees, presidents—are assigned their own particular kinds of roles, and there are strong pressures to force conformity to these roles.

The five essays of Part Four examine the structures of academic roles and suggest some ways that they might be discarded. Essays by two university presidents—John W. Ward (Chapter Sixteen) and Edward J. Bloustein (Chapter Seventeen)—present arguments that arrive at the same conclusion: While the principle of institutional neutrality in the political realm must be safeguarded, the university president who remains merely a role-player necessarily becomes something less than a person, for he loses his self. *These two authors speak directly from personal experience, and sensitive readers will respond to the high drama and suspense which the essays contain.*

The essay by Robert M. Diamond (Chapter Fifteen) attacks traditional conceptions of student and teacher roles. Diamond explores the central concept in educational innovation—the individualization of student learning. He describes the kind of curricular reform that will require the student to play a role that is now usually forbidden in schools. The student must become himself, *Diamond says, and the curriculum should fit the student's individual needs. The learning program for every student must be different.*

The opening and closing essays of Part Four brilliantly complement one another as they deal with the most troubling problem of all, the pluralistic ideal in education. Both Bernstein and Shoben defend this ideal, but they maintain that counterforces, existing both inside and outside the academic world, keep it from being realized. Bernstein argues that even where pluralism is realized on a campus, it must fail in its objectives because the job market cannot accommodate its graduates. If pluralism is to work within the educational realm, he says, then it must first be accepted by the whole of society— which has not yet been the case. Shoben demonstrates how our traditional concept of "academic standards"—the system by which students are admitted into programs, by which their progress is judged, and which finally certifies successful completion—violates the principles of pluralism.

All in all, the reader will find nothing in the literature of higher education during the year 1973 that is more provocative or more profound than the essays of Part Three and Part Four of this volume.

JOSEPH AXELROD

℞ 14 ℞

Pluralism: Myths and Realities

Alison R. Bernstein

℞℞℞℞℞℞℞℞

I want to present two case studies of two quite different educational institutions and how they have responded to the concept of pluralism. First, the experience of Vassar College, when confronted recently with establishing a partially pluralistic curriculum, namely black studies and woman's studies programs; and, second, Staten Island Community College, where there has never been a repression of pluralism, and where the issue is how a pluralistic educational environment can plug into a society which does not share that institution's educational philosophy. I'm hoping that an examination of these "social laboratories," and their involvement with putting pluralism into practice, will illuminate what I consider to be a fundamental problem facing higher education. It is difficult, if not impossible, to advocate

131

pluralism in an educational setting without first looking at the kind of society these students are being asked to survive in.

Certain phrases acquire academic currency, get bandied about at faculty meetings, and show up as the titles of academic conferences. A few catch-phrases of yesteryear, the golden oldies of academia, include: independent programs, student power, black studies, internships and, of course, relevance. The term *pluralism* has acquired that faddishness. I suppose that most people would simply define pluralism as a concept which allows for more than one variable, approach, or solution. This definition rarely takes into account whether the variables, approaches, and solutions are accorded equal value and status. Furthermore, when educators discuss pluralism in a contemporary context, they are really talking about programs to augment already established educational systems. Pluralism has become an afterthought —a new justification for accommodating previously excluded students into college classrooms.

To get an historic definition of the concept of pluralism, I sought out Horace Kallen, who, at the age of 90, is still actively teaching philosophy at the New School. A student of Dewey and William James, Kallen emerged a half century ago as one of the leading spokesmen for the school of Cultural Pluralism. In 1915, Kallen formulated the classic statement on pluralism: "As in an orchestra, every type of instrument has its special timbre and tonality, found in its substances and form; as every type has its appropriate theme and melody in the whole symphony, so in society each ethnic group is a natural instrument, its spirit and culture are its theme and melody, and the harmony and dissonances and discords of them all make the symphony of civilization."[1] Implicit in this concept of pluralism is an acknowledgment that no single life style or world view can be imposed by one group upon others.

Now, let me turn to Vassar College for a moment. One hundred and twelve years ago Vassar was founded in the midst of the Civil War by a Poughkeepsie brewer who wanted "to give women an education opportunity equal to that of Yale and Harvard." Roughly translated, this has meant that for the last hundred and eight years, Vassar has lived up to Matthew Vassar's ambitious hopes by preparing the Anglo-Saxon female either for marriage to a member of the Anglo-Saxon male elite or for a life of spinsterly careerism. Of course there

[1] Horace M. Kallen, "Democracy Versus the Melting Pot," *The Nation*, 100 (Feb. 18, 1915), p. 220.

were a number of "ethnics" in the student body, a few less among the faculty, and hardly any on the board of trustees. When I was an undergraduate at Vassar, four light-years ago, they had yet to hire a Jew or a Catholic as a full-time teacher in the religion department of a supposedly non-sectarian school. Needless to say, our ecumenical chapel services have always been presided over by Protestant chaplains-in-residence. And when I, as the only Jew, was appointed to the board of trustees I suppose I was not particularly shocked to witness invocations from the Bible at the opening of our meetings. Like other good, private, liberal arts schools, Vassar prided itself on the diversity of its academic offerings—even though there was only a smattering of courses offered in the study of non-Western European culture and society. There were some history courses which dealt with the ancient and the medieval world, but always from the perspective of the modern European-American scholar. And somehow the history of Africa ended with the pharoahs, and the history of the Middle East, with the fall of Constantinople. But, I do not mean to disparage the Vassar curriculum for the first hundred years of its history; it served its student consumers very well. The school transmitted the knowledge the students needed to survive well in a world dominated by the white, male, Anglo-Saxon values which awaited them upon their graduation.

In the last four years, Vassar has successfully beaten back two serious challenges to its educational mission. The challenges came from blacks and women. At first glance the history of the involvement of the college with these two antagonists seems unrelated. Blacks had been historically excluded and women had been, historically, the college's raison d'être. But upon closer examination, it could be seen that blacks and women who were coming to Vassar in the late 1960s were encountering the same problem—that the historic orientation of the college was basically geared to a white, male, racist, and sexist society. True, it had always been educating women, but their education equipped them (with a few famous, conspicuous, exceptions) to find, as Elizabeth Janeway bluntly puts it, "a woman's place in a man's world." The blacks found that they were merely being accepted into a white world characterized by a benign neglect of their unique identities and academic needs.

To dramatize their situation, the black students on campus moved swiftly and aggressively. Vassar suffered its first sit-in in the fall of 1969. The students' demands included: the creation of a black and urban studies center, a chance for black students to voluntarily live together on campus, and the addition of black faculty and black studies courses to counterbalance a lily-white faculty and curriculum. Eventually, the college acceded to all of the demands. A black studies program was inaugurated by administrative fiat with a bewildered faculty voting its consent. The program was launched and new part-time black faculty members were hired. Courses were offered on Afro- and American experiences. The college rented an old building in downtown Poughkeepsie so that black students would have a means of communicating with their community. And, finally, the college pro- vided the option of separate housing for black students as far as the law allowed. In short, even though the program never received the status of a legitimate academic department, the college had finally acknowledged that it owed its black students a partially pluralistic environment at Vassar. Typically, they could still take Music 140—a survey course of the Western classical music tradition—but at least they had the option of considering non-Western musical forms.

For the next two years, there was relatively smooth sailing. Blacks on campus were exercising their limited options. Often these options included choosing to live together. This housing arrangement was dubbed "separatist" by most whites on campus, and it soon be- came evident that Vassar's concept of pluralism really meant, "be yourself on our terms, not your own." However, despite the private discomfort of the college with these sanctioned arrangements for black students, little resistance was given to letting black students do their own thing. Privately, administrators nursed hopes that once the desire of blacks for their own program reached its apex, a counter-revolu- tionary desire would arise from the black community to once again opt for a place in the white world. Those hopes were dashed last spring, when a new generation of black student leaders demanded a series of reforms which shook up the Vassar establishment. Basically these demands represented, "a separate administrative structure for black students—a college within a college."[2] Obviously, Vassar could not condone this kind of pluralism. Not even the more enlightened liberals on the Board had intended to push the college that far to- wards acknowledging such an arrangement for blacks. And so with the kind of swiftness and aggressiveness displayed by the black students in their takeover, the President and the Board passed a series of reso- lutions which had the effect of reversing this dangerous trend. The key

[2] Alan Simpson, "Report of the President" (January 1, 1971–October 1, 1972), unpublished manuscript, Vassar College Records, pp. 5–7.

concept embodied in the resolutions was that "Vassar's commitment to minority students is based on a philosophy of equal treatment for all students within the framework of a *unified* college."[3] (The italics are mine.) Black Studies was to be reorganized at Vassar along the lines of other academic interdisciplinary departments. In that way traditional academic standards of curricula development and faculty competence would reassert themselves. Faculty would hold joint appointments with other departments, thereby assuring the administration that there would be but one way to hire teachers (with Ph.D.s) and disseminate knowledge (with the appropriate "objectivity" of the patrician scholar). This whole incident raises a raft of questions with regard to pluralism. But before discussing them, let me dwell briefly on the issue of woman's studies at Vassar.

The conflict over woman's studies at Vassar was hardly as dramatic or as complex in its resolution. Over the past few years, a small but vocal number of women on campus have pointed to the relative paucity of courses dealing with the history and activities of women in our society. Last semester the college offered only four courses which could be legitimately called woman's studies. The few students who expressed an interest in majoring in woman's studies were discouraged by the academic counseling they received. They were told quite emphatically that Vassar had no intention of establishing a separate woman's studies department or major, despite the fact that a number of schools with far less impressive pseudofeminist credentials had already done so. If these women wanted to major in woman's studies they would have to devise an "independent" major through a regular department advisor or go somewhere else. When a trustee committee on women, on which I served, held hearings on strengthening Vassar's academic and social commitment to women, we were accused of undermining Vassar's coeducational image. The hope cherished by the feminists at Vassar of establishing a pluralistic perspective on the sexes has not been realized. Time and time again women were told that woman's studies is not an academically justified discipline because it doesn't have a methodology of its own and, more pragmatically, because it doesn't equip students with the skills to get a job. Of the two arguments presented to defend Vassar's failure to see the need for woman's studies, I find the latter quite interesting. The idea that a discipline must have some residual occupational value has also been a

3 Simpson, pp. 5–8.

great obstacle to the creation of black studies programs. Even at Vassar where a student could major in black studies, all black students were encouraged to create *joint* majors between black studies and a more "respectable" discipline. Needless to say, Vassar has never questioned the market-value of an English major or a history major. And since it does not perceive itself as a training school, I think the transparent reason for this emphasis on occupation is that Vassar essentially rejects the concept of a pluralistic educational environment.

Even with its three newest constituencies, blacks, women-centered-women, and men, the essence of a Vassar education continues to be the preparation of its graduates for society as it is. Vassar knows all too well that pluralism is a term which describes the external behavior habits of the public at large. But the corridors of power in America continue to be frequented by white upper-class and upper middle-class American males. So if Vassar chooses to admit ethnics, blacks, and women's libbers, the best service it can do for them is to provide them with the tools to find a niche in that world. When you are educating the so-called elite, there is no room for more than one approach, let alone espousing the equality of different approaches. Kallen's metaphor comparing a pluralistic society to a symphony orchestra, and the existence of each culture as a different choir in the orchestra with a different timbre and a different part to play, is interpreted at Vassar to mean, "let the other colleges educate the second fiddlers, we're interested in the conductors!" The sociological term for the academic menu served up by Vassar College to its student clientele is Anglo-Conformity and, as Andrew Gordon has suggested, "Anglo-Conformity in various guises has probably been the most pervasive ideology of assimilation in the American historical experience."[4]

Staten Island Community College is about as old as its youngest freshman, and yet it is the senior community college in the City University of New York system. It has moved from a gloomy office building overlooking the docks and piers of New York harbor to a greenbelt campus atop Todt Hill, on some of Staten Island's most desirable real estate. In the past decade, the student enrollment of SICC has grown ten fold. Three factors contributed to this phenomenon: the bridge, open admissions, and Bill Birenbaum. The bridge, the Verrazano-Narrows which linked the tight little island to the

---

[4] Milton Gordon, "Assimilation in America: Theory and Reality," in Peter I. Rose, ed., *The Study of Society* (New York: Random House, 1970), pp. 409–425.

Brooklyn-Queens expressway, opened up the borough to the masses from the mainland and forever sealed the fate of Staten Island with the future of New York City. Open admissions guaranteed a place in the City University for any student with an "earned" high school degree. This meant that even if there was no problem of overcrowding at SICC, students from the Bronx, Brooklyn, and Manhattan might find themselves assigned to our community college. Finally, when one talks about the growth of SICC, one has to mention Bill Birenbaum. As president of the school, he has been responsible for generating programs which have resulted in the growth in numbers of black and Spanish-speaking students, veterans, adults returning for another chance, ex-addicts, college drop-outs, and open admissions candidates.

What does this brief analysis have to do with pluralism? At Staten Island Community College there is an infinite variety of programs geared to help those students *identify* their own academic needs and personal goals. It is no coincidence that at President Birenbaum's inauguration one of the guests of honor was Horace Kallen. In the curriculum, in the student body (the only ethnic group conspicuously absent at SICC is the WASP), in the hiring of faculty and administrators, there is a conscious desire to demonstrate a pluralistic awareness and a respect for the diversity of human experience. When I attend meetings of the board of trustees at Vassar and inevitably hear the cry that there are just not enough "qualified" minority group professionals, I just have to laugh. At SICC they have had little problem in finding people with top-flight talent to administer programs and teach classes. Perhaps these professionals know that there is a chance to exert influence and authority at SICC that a token job at Vassar could never give them. And if there is any "establishment" to be found at SICC, it is a black and Jewish male coalition. But even this is in the process of transition as women and white ethnics are pulling their ideas and aspirations together. But to talk of pluralism in higher education is to really discuss the alternative educational opportunities offered students in any one environment.

At SICC, the academic menu is a smorgasbord of main courses. There is the traditional curriculum offering the associate in arts degree, and there is training in the technologies. Although I do not teach in these areas, I am told that SICC holds its own with the best technological institutes in all forms of vocationally oriented training. And then there are the "other colleges" within SICC's walls. Taken together they begin to sound like an academic New Deal. Their titles belie their approach: College Discovery, Circle 73, the University Without Walls, Special Admissions, The Place, The Community Scholars Program, The Fort Dix Program for returning Vets, the CUNY/BA, Woman's Studies, the Urban Studies Learning Center, the Performing and Creative Arts Learning Center, and the list continues. Although none of the programs were specifically designed to ghetto-ize a particular group within its walls, all seem to have attracted a self-selected clientele. College Discovery recruits students who are not only unable to pay the small college fees (tuition in the City University, notwithstanding Governor Rockefeller, remains free), but who need a living stipend so that they can go to school fulltime, instead of having to work fulltime to support their families after high school graduation. Two-thirds of these students are black and Puerto Rican. The Fort Dix program has been overwhelmingly black, as is the Special Admissions program (a program designed for ex-addicts). The Circle 73 and Place programs cater primarily to white ethnics who were disillusioned with the education they were receiving in the "straight" college and, even more importantly, were conscious of the ways that the course of study was "programing" them into lower-middle-class white- and blue-collar anonymity. They were the kids who were supposed to passively sink into an educational and career shaft which promised little in the way of social or economic mobility. They are Patricia Cross's "New Students": the low-ability, non-traditional students from anti-intellectual environments with negative self-images accumulated through years of academic failure,[5] except that at Staten Island, these "new students" are suddenly being turned on to micro-economics instead of business technology, and Marx instead of Auto Mechanics Manuals, and they are proving their intellectual competence to survive in an academic setting. Obviously their abilities had not been discovered in twelve years of lower-class education.

There is nothing wrong with studying auto mechanics or business technology, as long as the society which is being served by these "professionals" values their expertise, and their selfhood, as much as it values its doctors, lawyers, and bankers. However, there is nothing inherent in the genes of a working class kid that makes him more suited to fixing cars, and in those of a Boston Brahmin that makes him more adept at repairing limbs. The type-casting of white working-class ethnics as basically trainable but "uneducable" students is under

---

[5] See K. Patricia Cross, *Beyond the Open Door* (San Francisco: Jossey-Bass, 1971).

attack at SICC. In a pluralistic educational environment, there is no single approach to learning, to the development of skills, to the course of study one pursues, or, ultimately, to the kind of self-actualizing person one becomes. In many ways Staten Island Community College has become a normless, pan-cultural society, which is not to say that there are no academic standards or standards of personal behavior at SICC. There are, but they are in the context of mutual respect and the law. The orchestration of pluralism at SICC is not without its dissonances and sharps and flats. But basically the disparate cultural constituencies coexist—the gays and straights, whites and non-whites, feminists and non-feminists, Spanish-speaking and non-Spanish-speaking, the medical technicians and the Marxist theoreticians—and they are all being educated according to their needs and expectations.

It would be easy to hold up the Staten Island version of pluralism as a model for institutions to follow, and many of the more zealous younger faculty members are trying to turn SICC into a four-year liberal arts college—the Swarthmore of Staten Island. However, there is one serious flaw in this otherwise idyllic picture of what pluralism ought to be in education. The easiest way to say it is that the world is not ready for it, nor, I'm afraid, for its students.

If Vassar perceives as indistinguishable its educational and its social function—the training of an elite—the same cannot be said for Staten Island Community College. SICC's educational philosophy, embodied in a pluralistic approach to student needs and societal expectations, is at loggerheads with its social function—specifically to grant terminal degrees in the training of middle-management technocrats, and to serve as an academic jungle where only the fittest (by whose standards?) survive the two-year crunch and are given the privilege of attending a somewhat more prestigious senior college. And so when some tenured member of some staid old department decries as unrealistic the efforts of the college to provide alternative educational opportunities to students, he is probably correct. Some faculty members insist that instead of teaching women about Elizabeth Cady Stanton, which may raise their consciousness but not their salaries, the college should be teaching advanced stenography. Anyway, it is hard to refute the charge that the education provided at SICC may be dysfunctional for many of the students. Anyone who knows what job market awaits SICC graduates shudders at the thought of leading them on to think that there is a seat on the floor of the stock exchange awaiting them instead of a typing table at some insurance company.

Yet, the answer is not to abandon the student-oriented curriculum, scrapping it for the perpetuation of a class-oriented system of education. As Birenbaum has written in his book, *Overlive,* "the issue in the country is stratification."[6] I'd like to amend that thought further. The issue in education is also stratification. As long as community colleges cater solely to one strata of the population—the have nots—no amount of pluralistically inspired educational philosophy, good will, and hard work will substantially alter the bleak future awaiting SICC's graduates.

Having painted this essentially pessimistic picture of the pitfalls of putting pluralism in higher education, I am still unwilling to abandon the concept. As G. K. Chesterton once said of another noble ideal, Christianity, "pluralism is not a bad thing, its just never been tried!" For pluralism to have any meaning as a viable educational philosophy, we need nothing short of a reconstruction of our society. Where is this reconstruction coming from? The mythology of traditional higher education suggested that social changes would emanate from within the "value-free" walls of the Ivory Towers. But the curious paradox I have here uncovered is that the educational establishment as typified by the Vassar experience has never resided *behind* ivy-covered walls. Its value system and approach to minorities in society has merely reflected and supported the "popular passions." The supposed detachment of traditional academic institutions belies their real attachment to the most strongly-held beliefs of our society. They have bought the system, while declaring their objectivity about it. If America continues to pursue a class-oriented, Anglo-conforming vision of its "perfect" society, the future of places like Vassar will be secure. If the demand for the restructuring of our society is met by the tightening of government surveillance over our lives and liberties, the elitist academic institutions will continue to supply government and industry with its leadership pool. These leaders will not rock the boat, or bow to the winds of equalitarianism and pluralism.

On the other hand, if the revolutionary consciousness which found its way onto college campuses and television screens in the 1960s surfaces again in the plight of third-world people, women, gays, returning veterans, draft resisters, and even lower class white ethnics, then places like Vassar will be in for a rough time, and institutions like Staten Island Community College will stand as nascent, experi-

---

[6] William Birenbaum, *Overlive: Power, Poverty and the University* (New York: Delta Books, 1969), p. 160.

mental models which have challenged the status quo. The curious paradox about the Staten Island experience is that it has never claimed distance from the so-called real world. As a community college, it has always interpreted its role as to serve a broadly-based constituency. The administration has always adopted a political approach to the solution of SICC's problems. And yet, for all its mucking about in the real world, SICC has devised an educational philosophy which points to a new equalitarian and pluralistic ordering of society. If a reconstruction of society takes place, Staten Island Community College will continue to function as a signpost, marking the evolution of a pluralistic environment.

It would be easy to end here. But a more complex question has yet to be asked. Assuming the creation of a pluralistic society, how can our educational institutions handle distinctions based on talent in a truly equalitarian setting? Another way of asking this question is, "How do we as educators honor excellence within a pluralistic institution without creating new elites?" It is one thing to call for the creation of a new equality of life styles and of values, it is quite another to permit room for individual differences to assert themselves without creating new kinds of stratification. This is the next topic on the agenda at Staten Island Community College, and, I dare say, the most pressing one for pluralists throughout the country. Unless we address ourselves to the diversity of human abilities as well as human experiences, we have only half completed our tasks as educators. To be a pluralist is to see and to know that the melting pot did not melt, and there is little use trying to revive that tired image. Each of us has our own pot, thank God. In a pluralistic society, education must help us learn the best use of it.

$\mathfrak{X}15\mathfrak{X}$

Individualizing
Student Learning

Robert M. Diamond

$\mathfrak{X}\mathfrak{X}\,\mathfrak{X}\mathfrak{X}\,\mathfrak{X}\mathfrak{X}\,\mathfrak{X}\mathfrak{X}\,\mathfrak{X}\mathfrak{X}\,\mathfrak{X}\mathfrak{X}\,\mathfrak{X}\mathfrak{X}\,\mathfrak{X}\mathfrak{X}$

$\mathbb{A}$cademic innovation is possible in higher education but it does not happen by chance. Major changes occur only when procedures and human resources are combined to generate a climate in which innovation is not only permitted but encouraged. The process is difficult, to say the least, and often far more complex than many faculty and administrators first anticipate. It is my intention to describe here a process for academic change that has been in operation at Syracuse University for the past two years. I will record what has happened as a result, with emphasis on what worked, what didn't work, and the reasons why.

It is essential to view the Syracuse Project in perspective. Much of what exists today as the structure and process of higher education is based on 19th-century educational concepts. We have an academic structure which equates achievement with contact hours and tends to look at students as part of a vaguely defined group rather than as individuals. In reality, however, no two students are alike. They enter a college or university with different backgrounds, different interests, different priorities, different abilities, and, very often, different learning styles. We must, if we are to succeed in teaching them, design a program that is sensitive to their differences. We must individualize our academic programs.

Unfortunately, the word *individualization* has become one of those terms that mean just about anything from mere independent study to increased faculty-student contact. As a concept, individualization is so multi-dimensional that few programs totally accomplish it. For example, although both the Keller Plan and the audiotutorial approach are excellent management systems, they do not represent completely individualized instruction.

If an instructional program is truly individualized, it must include six essential elements: (1) A flexible time frame which permits each student to progress through the program as rapidly as he can and, at the same time, meet pre-stated instructional goals. (2) Both remedial assignments and unit exemptions which are based on a student's entering knowledge and competencies. (3) Content options which are based on a student's individual interests or major field of study. (4) A choice of locations for instructional elements that need not be confined to campus, including the dormitory, home, library, and community as places for learning. (5) A wide variety of appropriate techniques and time flexibility in evaluating a student's progress. (6) A choice, so far as is feasible, of instructional styles.

As we explore the ramifications of individualization, we become increasingly aware that the impact on higher education can be far more extensive than we might have first expected, requiring, for example, some major changes in administrative procedures. At Syracuse, individualization has already resulted in flexible-credit courses and continual registration, and in fall, 1973, courses began to be offered for University credit as a regular part of high school curriculums. The effect of these programs upon the registrar and room-scheduling offices has been, to say the least, traumatic. And yet without their full cooperation as well as the assistance of other administrative units of the University, much of the instructional innovation would have been impossible.

Academic change requires adjustments in the overall academic structure. More and more we find that credit options within courses are being shared by departments which cooperatively offer courses and minicourses. These programs not only create challenging logistical problems for the registrar's office but generate some fundamental questions concerning academic loads and assignment of appropriate credit to the cooperating departments. Solutions can become quite complex. For example, a new flexible-credit course on drugs, offered by the School of Social Work and attracting an enrollment in excess of four hundred students, actively involves the following diverse elements: the Syracuse University College of Law, the School of Management, the Department of Religion, the School of Public Communications, the Upstate Medical Center (a part of the State University of New York), a local radio station, community drug agencies, and the city police department. When this course is viewed in its broadest perspective, its position becomes quite intriguing. Some highly volatile questions are raised in attempts to decide which department should be entitled to credit toward faculty load.

Individualization also has impact on the faculty, the student, and the resources that are utilized. A faculty member finds himself spending less time lecturing and more in small group and counseling situations. He may find that he has opportunity to spend a greater percentage of effort in his area of specialization, especially in teaching short, three-to-five week instructional segments. The student finds, in individualized programs, that he must accept more responsibility for his own learning, and the program planners find that the course structure itself must help the student through the transition from rigidity to flexibility.

As more emphasis is placed on independent study and on less-regimented time frames, there is an increasing need to use inexpensive, modular instructional materials such as programed booklets, manuals, audio tapes, etc. The more expensive but less flexible techniques of film and television should be considered when a combination of sound and movement is essential. Greater flexibility of instruction is accompanied by increased use of independent learning laboratories as well as greater reliance on the reserve desk of the library. It is essential to emphasize that closely prescribed structure and individualization are not mutually exclusive characteristics. In fact, it is becoming increasingly apparent that an effective program of individualization must be highly structured if the necessary operational elements which include options, remedial units, and exemptions are to function effectively. As flexibility increases, so must the basic structure of the program be increased.

Before any program of academic redesign is undertaken, those responsible for both the establishment and operation of the project must be aware that sooner or later they must answer the question, Is it worthwhile? The answer involves the "accountability cycle" and is composed of three elements: *Cost benefit analysis,* which involves establishing priorities among goals. *Cost effectiveness analysis,* which relates expenditures to results. *Accountability,* which relates results to the established priorities.

Of the three areas, it is in the second that most problems occur because of the tendency to answer the question of cost effectiveness in rather simplistic terms by looking solely at the student-faculty ratio. In reality, cost effectiveness is far more complex than that and must be investigated in terms of students, faculty, physical space, academic learning, time periods, and community relations. For example, if we reduce the dropout or failure rate of an academic program, we improve our cost effectiveness. If we increase the scope of learning that takes place, or reduce the time required to meet a specific objective, or increase retention, or generate more academic credits with the same resources, we improve cost effectiveness. The ability to handle more students with the same resources is obviously an improvement in cost effectiveness but so are the following: an increase in direct student-faculty contact, the ability of a faculty member to spend a greater amount of his time in his field of specialization, and the capability of a faculty member to add to his own field of knowledge. We also improve our cost effectiveness if we use space more efficiently, increase the utilization of existing resources such as libraries and community facilities, and improve the attitudes of the public toward our institution. If our graduates are better qualified to meet their job requirements and if a smaller percentage of our graduates are unemployed or misemployed, we also meet the criteria for improved cost effectiveness.

It becomes critical, therefore, that we resist the urge to measure the work of any project by a single criterion because, when we do, there is a tendency to reach the wrong conclusions. What good is it, for example, to handle more students at the same cost if students are antagonized and the curriculum is irrelevant and poorly taught? How successful is a program that has a 20, 30 or even 50 percent dropout or failure rate? It is essential that, at the very beginning of a project, every effort be made to generate data that will help establish that the project is worthwhile. The question will surely be asked and we must be ready to answer it.

Higher education, if it is to continue to exist as we know it, must provide each student with an academic program that meets his needs and, simultaneously, the needs of the community. The problem is greatest for private institutions because they must excel in quality of instruction and advantageous campus climate in order to compete with the less expensive state systems. Success in this competition requires change: change in structure, change in curricula, and change in process. These will not occur without the full support and hard dollar commitment of the administration and the cooperation of the faculty on whom the responsibility for instruction rests. Change is urgently needed. It can take place through the careful and effective utilization of resources that are presently available.

16

The College
President as Citizen

John William Ward

W hether college presidents should take stands on sensitive
public issues is an important and complex question. It is not readily
answered, because it *is* important and complex—and not just to college presidents. If that were the case, one might surrender to the impulse to give the question a short answer. But it is important to all
institutions, not just to institutions of higher education; and the question is complex because it draws in its train central questions about
the meaning and the conduct of our common political life.

Let me rephrase the question to make what is at issue more
stark. "Should a *citizen* take a stand on a sensitive public issue?" I
suppose we would all affirmatively nod our heads if the question were
put that way, because in a society such as ours, power finds its ultimate sanction in the consent of the people in whose name and interest

147

ideally, a least, that power is wielded. For the exercise of power to be legitimate in a free society, the citizen must be free to think and speak, and free to act politically. We are, rightly enough, appalled at political cultures which call themselves democratic because they hold periodic plebiscites in which the people are allowed the privilege only of saying yes. We do not count a society free unless the citizen has an uninhibited voice in the process of finding answers to sensitive public issues. So, a citizen should take a stand: political and moral responsibility lie behind that "should." A political community which accepts a government and its policies, and the actions necessary to effect those policies, bears a collective responsibility for the actions of its government. Further, a man continuing to accept membership in the political community derives a personal and individual share of that collective responsibility. That is why a citizen should take a stand on sensitive public issues. The citizen must, if our ideals are to be realized in action and not just celebrated in rhetoric.

What happens to the clarity of that answer when one asks "should a college president take a stand?" If one feels, as I do, hesitation in giving a short and clear answer to the question in this form, is it not because one senses that the institutional role must, by its nature, somehow inhibit the citizen who plays it? The answer is indubitably yes, the citizen inhibited by the role.

I have discovered that simple fact in my own life. In spring, 1972, my first in office as president of Amherst College, I was arrested for an act of passive civil disobedience in protest against the conduct of the war and the United States policy in Vietnam. In a talk to students and faculty on the campus, however, I drew a sharp distinction between my office, my role as president, and my self—what I intended to do as citizen. As president, I insisted then, and still insist, that I did not intend to turn the college into a political and social instrument and would not allow anyone or any group to do so. I insisted that as President I would always act to preserve the space for freedom, for difference of opinion, for each and every voice to be heard on the campus, because of my commitment to the principle that education requires a setting free from coercion in any form.

I then shifted into my voice as a single citizen and gave the reasons why I chose to engage in an act of civil disobedience. I tried, in other words, to maintain the distinction between my self and my role. Pragmatically, it worked; that is, faculty and students (with some exceptions) understood the dilemma in which I found myself and respected, or at least tolerated, the distinction I wished to maintain. The public, however, did not. Curiously, both supporters and critics rejected the distinction. Those who supported my action wrote that I should recognize that I am president because of the person I am, and that I should use the prestige of my office as a platform to advance my own ideas. Those who attacked my action wrote that once I had accepted the office I had foregone the privilege of acting as an individual citizen, because the public would identify anything I said or did as the voice of Amherst College and not the voice of Bill Ward. I found myself, and still find myself, in a dilemma. I do not want to use the institution of which I am proud to be the president as an extension of my self; neither do I wish to accept the fact that the institutional role I must play means the obliteration of my self.

All of which is to say that I am not wholly satisfied with the distinction between two voices, one as president, one as citizen. I am willing to try to maintain the distinction until I can find a better and more intellectually satisfying answer to the question, and I wish to explore the dilemma by way of a tentative search for a better answer.

The president of a college does not speak as a single, private, individual citizen. Whether he will or no, others attend to what a president says precisely because of the assumption that the role, the office of college president, gives the citizen who holds it some special competence or authority to speak. If that were a general competence rather than a special competence, we would have an easy answer to the question: the greater the competence, the greater the responsibility to speak out. If people do believe that college presidents are by virtue of their office especially worth attending to, then college presidents have a special reason to speak out. However, one suspects that the answer most anticipated is that, yes, college presidents have a special competence, competence in the affairs of education, and they should restrict themselves to the area of their competence and not use the aura of their office to speak on unrelated matters, however pressing, however sensitive.

There is considerable force to such an answer, but also a considerable problem. Let me, though, give the force its full weight. If Kingman Brewster, President of Yale, say, writes a letter to the *New York Times,* and even if he asserts that he speaks only for himself, the *Times* will print and the public will read what he says in large measure because he is president of a prestigious university. This would seem to require some tact on the part of any president in choosing when to speak. Tact is a personal virtue, however, and provides no objective guide. If one follows the guide that one should speak only on matters which affect the vitality of the educational process, because that is one's domain, the guide leads rather quickly onto treacherous ground.

I would have no hesitation, for example, in speaking out strongly against any movement in society which would erode first amendment freedoms, for the obvious reason that freedom of speech is essential to the openness which makes an educational institution possible at all. The First Amendment is one way to define the essence of education. But as one moves away from such clear and unambiguous ground, the path becomes less firm. It would not take a casuist to argue that the maldistribution of income today in the United States affects the vitality of education itself. For caution's sake, let me insist that I am not talking about social justice, I am talking about education. I do not think that educational institutions should become a microcosm of the general society, but I do think an educational institution should be intent on fostering as great a variety as possible among its intellectually qualified members in order to bring the richest possible variety of personal experience and social perspective to bear upon the educational process which takes place in it.

All of which is to say that the answer that college presidents should confine themselves to issues which affect education is not terribly helpful in providing an unambiguous answer to the question before us. It simply sets the president the task of tracing as best as he can the consequences for education of an issue, and if it is truly sensitive, the odds are high that one will be able to trace a line of filiation from the issue to education itself.

But beyond not being terribly helpful, the answer that one's function in an institution, one's role as president, inhibits the exercise of one's general responsibility as a citizen has a terrible consequence lurking in it. The liberal notion that the body politic consists of free and single individuals who, by speaking out on public issues, arrive at a democratic consensus, is not only grandly optimistic in its assumption of rationality, it is also terribly abstract and unrelated to the concrete realities of our social and political life.

One night, as I checked into a monster of a hotel to attend a convention on this very issue, I was in the registration line long enough to get into deep conversation with the man behind me. (If the wait had been a bit longer, I think that we might have had the basis for a life-long friendship.) We finally found our way to who I was and why

I was there. He remarked, "As a citizen, I *care* about such things, but I have a job. I don't get involved." My response was that since most people had jobs, the public was in bad shape, wasn't it? At least, his position offered the only *political* argument I have heard against full employment. A chance encounter, but it puts anecdotally what I want to say at greater length about the consequence of insisting that one has responsibilities as a citizen, but is inhibited from acting on them by the demands of one's position in an institution.

If one generalizes the proposition, the public vanishes. As I said, many have told me that I had foregone the privilege to act as an individual when I took the office of president because the public would not understand the distinction between my self and my role. The public probably will not, but now follow the logic of the other horn of the dilemma. The individual cannot speak because he may involve the institution in which he lives part of his life, whether that institution be a college, a church, or a corporation. The college president, the officer of a corporation, anyone who holds a job cannot speak because he may implicate the institution of which he is a part. So, one turns to the institution and gets the answer that each has a special function in our complex society, education, banking, whatever. The institution cannot take a stand on matters of general public, political, and moral concern. It is not, as we say, their business. When one asks, "Who is responsible?" it turns out there is no one there to answer the question. The result is precisely the frustration, alienation, and anomie which lead either to a cynical privatism or sudden outbursts of mass action. There are no constituted ways to address the very problems which are most important to all citizens.

I think that the major item on our political agenda is to ask the difficult question how we might extend the idea of citizenship from the single self to the anonymous institutions which characterize our society and which exercise power in it. That is, as I say, a difficult question. Until we have the will to address it and the imagination to answer it, at the very least let us not surrender our own selves to our jobs; let us not say that we cannot listen to our own minds and consciences, but must wait upon the collective personality of whatever institution it may be, which we also then say must be voiceless.

The dilemma I have tried to explore is a true dilemma in the sense that either side of it leads to an untenable extreme. I do not wish to accept the logical consequence of either side of the dilemma when carried to its logical conclusion. Must I rest then in a contradiction? I hope not, because my own sense of history is that when a society confronts a question and puts the question to itself in such a way that the only answers forthcoming are unacceptable, that society is at bottom trying to justify social existence as it is. That is, the society is unwilling to transcend the present, but wishes to affirm it as necessary. To put it another way, one suspects a strong conservative impulse if all answers to a question prove to be untenable.

When individuals in a society say that they recognize certain social injustices but, unhappily, because of their location in society cannot speak or act on their perceptions, then one suspects that the sense of powerlessness, however much deplored, is preferred over the necessity to transform the social reality. To put it in less abstract language, the society has lost the political will to achieve social justice. There are no sensitive public issues because there is no public.

If that be the case, and one will, of course, recognize it as a description of the moment in which we find ourselves, in the guise of an argument, then what does it have to do with the question whether a college president should speak out on sensitive public issues? I think it has a great deal to do with it, and I think it dictates that college presidents have a special responsibility as educators to speak out on public issues for two reasons: first, for the vitality of the educational institution itself, and second, to fulfill the social function of the institution.

For the first, if one tells students, as I have for many years, that their education is not only to train their minds, but to prepare them to lead decent and humane lives in whatever social role their intelligence qualifies them for, one had better not implicitly teach them at the same time that it is not possible to act on that ideal. To remain mute and hide behind the fiction that one cannot speak precisely because one is an educator involves a contradiction of the purpose of education itself and negates the ancient ideal of liberal education.

For the second, the social function of education, I take it that one-half of the purpose of education as an institution is to act as a critic of the assumed and unquestioned values of society. If that is part of the purpose of the institution one heads, then the president cannot abdicate his responsibility to act on that purpose himself. To do so would, again, contradict the purpose of education itself.

Finally, though, there is a deeper reason why a college president should speak out on sensitive public issues. All institutions, but especially educational institutions, are a set of processes, not some objective structure. We tend to reify the process and call it Amherst College or what ever. We objectify it, and thus alienate ourselves from it. Institutions are not fixed entities; they are in a continual state of transformation into other forms. The name *Amherst College* has remained the same since 1821, but the reality it points to has changed remarkably in more than one hundred-fifty years. Of all people, the president should recognize that the essence of his own institution is the dialogue, the dialectic, if you will, by which the institution transcends its present state and maintains the vitality for growth and change. That process requires the courage to be critical of what is. The president must have that courage and act on it.

17

College Presidents as Political Activists

Edward J. Bloustein

To state my conclusion at the very outset, I believe very strongly that college and university presidents should express themselves on sensitive public issues—on issues of conscience, and on fundamental moral issues. I believe as well that the failure of many of my colleagues to do so was in a large measure responsible for the turmoil and chaos of our campuses in the sixties.

I recognize that a president who undertakes such a role as I suggest can jeopardize a fundamental principle of academic life—the political neutrality of our educational institutions. And this, too, is a principle to which I am very committed. If these beliefs leave me with an irreconcilable conflict, I can only say that I think it is a necessary and inevitable conflict. What is at issue here, as in so many instances of human choice, is the necessity of balancing two conflicting values.

154

If the president is appropriately sensitive to the threat his activism poses to institutional neutrality, I believe he can resolve the conflict and thereby serve the best interests of his conscience, his institution, and higher education generally.

There is a distinctly different set of problems relating to the activism of faculty and students, where I see little or no threat posed to the neutrality of the university. And there is also a different set of problems in relation to administrators other than the president within the university or college. Here the threat and the prospects of reconciling it are distinctly different from either the case of the president or of faculty and students. Therefore, I want to make it plain at the outset that my conclusions relate solely to the presidential figure.

Before going into the reasons for my own position, I want to say a word about the political neutrality of institutions. It seems a great shame to me that we rarely discuss this important issue when tempers and emotions are calm enough to discuss it rationally. All of the provocative discussions of institutional neutrality seem to take place when the immediate necessities and urgencies of our situation make it almost impossible to be objective about the matter. Looking back now from the relative calm of the seventies, I would like to consider two or three aspects of the principle of political neutrality.

First, I think we deceive ourselves and our students and faculty in using the term *political neutrality* as descriptive of American institutions of higher education, without clarifying for ourselves what we mean by it. Our institutions of higher education are wedded to political democracy and opposed to any form of totalitarianism; they are wedded to a political system that encourages political inquiry and opposed to one that threatens free inquiry. In that sense, we are not politically neutral at all. We are committed to a specific type of political system, one in which free inquiry finds protection as a fundamental value.

There is a second important respect in which the university is not neutral, and that concerns its efforts to influence political decisions which affect its very life. We have more people on Capitol Hill pressing our political position than most other industries in America. We are up to our knees, necks, and over our heads in any and every form of political influence at the federal level and certainly at the state level. I regularly meet with my legislators in New Jersey. I am not sure that it does any good, but I certainly attempt to influence them in every way I know how in respect to issues pertaining to education which are likely to come before them.

Finally, I think it would be less than honest, when we talk about the principle of political neutrality, not to recognize that most of the people who serve on boards of governors and boards of trustees in these United States—and most college and university presidents—are firmly wedded not only to political democracy, but to the economic and social status quo. Our institutions are not neutral in respect to the economic institutions of American life; in fact, whatever they say in theory, my board of governors is a quite conservative body devoted to quite conservative principles, and their principles intrude into the life of the university at every turn. It is, I believe, a deception, though not a conscious one, to say that our institutions are politically neutral in these terms. They are not. Most of them are very conservative institutions protecting the economic status quo.

When we talk about the political neutrality of institutions, I believe it is essential that we keep these exceptions in mind. We can speak only of degrees of neutrality or, conversely, of the appropriate limits of presidential activism. Even within this context I believe there is a conflict; and it is, as I have already said, a necessary conflict. I am going to give you a simple illustration. What many of us would hope for—that is, many of us in presidential positions—is that people would allow us to be human, allow us the same right to express opinion which students have, which faculty have, which most of the other members of our society have. We believe we can exercise this right by speaking as individuals, rather than as representatives of the institution. We are prepared to admit, however, that it is a pretty forlorn hope that we can ever really disassociate ourselves from our institution.

During the height of the anti-Vietnam movement, the difficulty of the president's disassociating himself from his political position was made manifest again and again. I received invitations from all kinds of political groups to speak, and I know that I would not have been tendered those invitations were it not for the fact that I was president of a college. I would always tell my hosts, "Look, I will speak personally, not as a representative of my college." And they would say, "Oh, yeah, we know what you mean." I am probably a second- or third-rate political thinker, and not much of an activist and not much of a speaker. They would not have wanted me if I were not president. They knew it, I knew it, and we were going through a charade of sorts in supposing I was speaking as an individual. No matter how many times you forswear institutional indentification on a public platform, the people who hear you think of you as an institutional representative, and as speaking for the institution.

Nevertheless, a president can limit that identification and limit the ill effects of it in very important ways if he is sensitive to it. In the first place, he should take every occasion to indicate that he is acting as an individual and not as a representative of an institution. Then he must do something even more difficult. He must protect those with whom he disagrees on the issue concerned. One of the great dangers of the president taking a position is that, for the students, faculty members, and administrators at his college, he begins to lose his identity as umpire, as protector of the rights of others on campus to speak freely. I saw this happen during my period at Bennington College when I took an anti-Vietnam War position. Those relatively more conservative members of the faculty and student body who were hesitant before I spoke out about coming to me to protect their rights were even less likely to come to me afterwards, because they thought, in view of the position I had taken, that I might not give them the full order of protection to which they were entitled. I was called upon to go out of my way to create special mechanisms and contexts to overcome this problem. I did not do it very well initially, but I learned as I went along. The circumstance of presidential activism necessitates the creation of a new structure which will afford protection.

Finally, it is extremely important for a president who takes a political position to protect against institutional funds and resources being used for the position. You can caution your administrators all you like. You can instruct them up and down the line. You can send out official notices that say, "This is an official notice from the president's office," and add on, "We really mean it," and then underscore, *We really mean it,* and the fact is that everyone is winking all the way down the line. Many of your junior administrators do not think you mean it. They think that when you put your shoulder to the political wheel, all of them ought to, and institutional resources ought to be moved in that direction.

Why, then, if the president's role as the neutral arbiter and protector of the rights of free inquiry of the institution is threatened by his taking a position, should he take it? I would like to cite three reasons which seem convincing to me. First, our universities and colleges have turned for the most part into moral wastelands in the postwar period. Because of the development of positivism in social sciences, scientism in the physical sciences, and a general loss of nerve in the intellectual community, the university has become a morally sterile place. Students and faculty facing the quandries of contemporary life yearn for a context in which moral discourse will become important again. I am not advocating a general moral position for the university or for the university president. Rather, I am suggesting that the university must be a place for the discussion of moral issues, a place where morals and ethics can be discussed by reasonable men. I believe that one of our great failures as institutions in the sixties was to abandon this very important role. The president, I think, in taking a position on sensitive issues, will help restore that role.

A second reason for presidential activism, it seems to me, is that we should want to attract to the presidencies of our colleges and universities men and women who would find it personally repugnant *not* to express their basic moral and political convictions. Some readers may know that in the early history of the Supreme Court of the United States, Chief Justice Marshall thought it very important that the dissenters on the court not issue dissenting opinions. The system broke down because the justices found it repugnant to remain silent. We should not choose Supreme Court judges who maintain personal silence on the basic issues of public policy and Constitutional law which come before the court. I would say, likewise, that we should not choose as presidents of educational institutions expressive of our basic humanistic values men and women who remain silent on the issues of conscience which come before the academic community.

The third reason I suggest that the president be an activist is that the politically neutral president comes to be perceived by the faculty and the student body as an ethical eunuch, and thereby limits his capacity to provide leadership. In some considerable measure, credibility and effectiveness as a collegiate leader depends on a president's personal characteristics, his warmth, his humanity, his sensitivity. Among those personal characteristics which constitute a touchstone of credibility is the president's sense of moral conviction. If stirring of conscience and ethical sensibility must be hidden under the bushel basket of neutrality, the president not only abdicates leadership on the particular moral issue, but also is subtly discredited in respect to all other aspects of his leadership.

In conclusion, I want to place two important limitations on what I have said. First, the presidential activism which I have been discussing is advocated only in relation to the most basic political and moral issues—only to issues of conscience. I do not suggest that the president become involved on a regular basis in partisan politics, either locally or nationally. I believe that would be a disaster.

Nor am I suggesting that the president become a daily fount of moral wisdom, a stump preacher of morals. It was only about forty or fifty years ago that my predecessor spoke in chapel every morning. I am not suggesting that presidents go back into the chapel pulpit.

With these limitations, and despite some dangers, I believe political activism in a president serves the college and university community well.

18

Academic Standards: A Problem in Values

Edward Joseph Shoben, Jr.

The substance of tragedy, it has been said, lies less in the conflict between good and evil than in the incompatability of good actions, good values, or good goals with each other. If that is the case, then at least the ingredients of tragedy loom before us in higher education in the tension between *academic standards* as we historically conceive them and the newer concepts of *pluralism* toward which many colleges and universities are sincerely but painfully attempting accommodations. Ideas of competence and the value of achievement lie deep in the American grain. But in the last decade, the consciousness of many has expanded to include two critical elements of awareness. One entails the recognition that large numbers of U.S. citizens have been excluded from opportunities to acquire competence and to register achievements simply by virtue of their ethnic, cultural, or sexual identity. The second consists in the perception that American culture comprises a variety of subcultures, that those subcultures simply do not (as the myth of the melting pot implied they would) homogenize in the crucible of a common societal experience, and that attaining any objective of human decency and fairness that transcends diversity requires that we somehow discover or create the conditions under which our differences can be celebrated and our distribution of de facto opportunities equalized. To serve this relatively new awareness, academic institutions have struggled to enroll populations that have always before been grossly underrepresented on their campuses and who emerge from backgrounds quite different from the sources from which more familiar kinds of students spring.

To the bewilderment and disappointment of many faculty members and academic administrators, these acts of good faith have produced little contentment and only questionable bases for pride. In more colleges than not, the admission of minorities and disadvantaged white students has produced conflict, bitterness, and failure. The reasons are obviously manifold and probably not completely identifiable. One crucial one, however, stands out sharply: cultural pluralism, an inherently egalitarian notion, collides head on with the inherently elite tradition of academic standards.

The issues here are many, complex, and thorny. I will touch on only three, but they are illustrative. The first has to do with the nature of the standards themselves; the second bears on the relationship of the standards not just to faculty members alone, but to academic persons generally; and the third centers on standards and one aspect of our modal institutional dynamics.

When we look first at the nature of academic standards, we are struck by four central features: an almost exclusive focus on symbolic abilities, a reliance on cognitive rationality as virtually the only acceptable epistemology, a closed and essentially self-contained system of standards, and the extent to which academic standards are used for sorting and certifying. Because as much clarity as we can muster is important here, we must examine each of these parameters of academic quality and their significance for the pluralism now being somewhat stumblingly sought after on many campuses.

It seems incontestable that symbolic proficiency lies at the heart of academic quality; and for most of us—especially for those of us who have walked long and happily in academic groves—this state of affairs appears eminently right. Language, including the language of quantities and the structures of abstract expression that we call theoretical science, is not only one of the fundamental and distinctive characteristics of man, it underlies almost all his triumphs in the course of his evolution and defines the prime tool by means of which he has solved his problems both individually and as a species. Viewed from this angle, the centrality of human symbolic functions in the pattern of academic values is of little wonder. Much would be lost if poetry, history, and mathematics were to disappear from the curriculum. There is no cause for surprise in the weight that has been attached to verbal and quantitative test scores in the development of admissions criteria. And the centering of graduation requirements in the demonstration of symbolic competence over a variety of substantive areas—the fields of concentration and distribution—strongly represents, whatever other rationales it may entail, an extension of this basic concern.

This basic concern is thoroughly legitimate, but it strikes a snag in relation to pluralistic aspirations. Although the capacity for symbolic activity is given by the species, actual symbolic skill must be learned, and the opportunities for that learning have been differentially spread over the subcultures of our society. In consequence, from the point of view of a college, good students are those who have most richly enjoyed the chance to hone their capabilities in reading, writing, listening, and conceptual speech; and the processes of society, sometimes in an ugly fashion, have concentrated such chances in significant measures among economically favored Caucasians. When students from other groups are admitted to collegiate halls in the name of pluralism, an unsavory set of alternatives is then posed: Either academic standards must be corrupted by dilution, or the members of these new clienteles must be subjected to both the humiliation and the expense of non-creditable remedial work. And the winds of trouble begin to blow in the groves of academe.

But the problem has still subtler and more far-reaching dimensions. Research by Guilford, Torrance, Taylor, and others indicate that there may be more than 120 relatively independent human abilities. As few as eight seem to be engaged by our typical educational exercises, and the patterning of this startling diversity of talents as they develop varies markedly from one subculture to another. The distinction made by ghetto blacks between "school smarts" and "street smarts" is one illustration of this point. The difference between the businessman's shrewdness and the scholar's intellectuality is a second.

The relatively low correlations between indices of standard academic achievement and measures of creativity are yet another. The number can be easily multiplied. The point is, that although there is no gainsaying the vital importance of symbolic capabilities, the range of human talents is surprisingly wide; and the focus in our educational enterprise on a narrow segment of that range may obscure one of the major virtues of pluralism, the contribution by one group to others of *abilities* that it has distinctively cultivated. In other words, because academic standards, as genuinely valuable as they are, are primarily standards of proficiency rather than of exploration and growth among a welter of talents, they achieve only a dubious applicability in a context of pluralism—a context that italicizes diversity.

The academic concern with symbolic functions shades into the academy's insistence on cognitive rationality as the epistemological basis for higher education. The proponents of the formal disciplines that define the curriculum historically and typically assume—they no longer have to argue the case if they ever did—that the overwhelmingly predominant if not the sole way of knowing, and hence of learning, consists in the manipulation by reason of cognitively acquired concepts and information. In a disciplinary context, it may well be so. But it is worth noting that one mode of knowing has become honored as the *only* mode of knowing. This observation enjoys connections with the evidence of a broader spectrum of human talents than most of us have typically attended to, and it pays little heed to philosophic specifications of other epistemological processes.

Josiah Royce, for example, took pains to identify not only rationality but intuition, empiricism, and authority as legitimate and vital—and perhaps inevitable—routes to personal and social understanding. A thinker as different as Henry David Aiken has, more recently, built a strong case for empathy and for moral, aesthetic, and religious "knowing" in the processes of significant learning. Whatever the very real assets of cognitive rationality, they rarely extend one's informed familiarity with such elements of life as form, color, and sequence, with the compexities of human feeling, or with the ways in which drives and emotions determine conduct and make demands upon it. When the methods of cognitive rationality attempt to deal with such intimate and often heated components of experience, they leave us with a sense of an empty and important gap between "knowing about" descriptively and "knowing" in a more unmediated and empathetically complex fashion. Parenthetically, this state of affairs is a rather curious one in an educational tradition in which "know thyself" is a central maxim.

Because the modes of knowing, the processes for achieving functional understanding, both vary from one subculture to another and extend beyond the boundaries of cognitive rationality, academic institutions have wrestled often and extensively in recent years with the question of how to introduce a larger element of experience into their programs that could better serve the interests of pluralism. Repeatedly, such efforts have willy-nilly translated the activities of learning into a somewhat simplistic duality of knowledge and experience, with the experiential side regarded as taking place outside the classroom and, indeed, off the campus. The conceptual inadequacies here pale before the practical difficulties. Field placements and internships become essentially jobs with only minor educational benefits. They become disassociated from classroom antecedents that might sharpen a student's perceptiveness or enlarge the angle of his observations and awareness; and they become divorced from those on-campus opportunities for informed reflection on one's experience, or the sharing of observations from different subcultural perspectives, that would directly capitalize on the principles of pluralism. Here again, there may be little reason for surprise. Even sympathetic faculty members and administrators, trained as exponents of the academic disciplines, rarely possess the skills, the insights, or the deeply informed concerns to permit their functioning effectively in this kind of milieu.

The nature of academic standards—the closed system that they define, and their function as a sorting and certifying device—may be quickly dealt with. The tales that must be told are now familiar ones, although they merit retelling. Two well-substantiated, but massively neglected, observations should be made regarding the expression of academic standards in the form of grades. One deals with what grades are related to; the other is concerned with what they reflect.

Perhaps the most widely shared notion of academic standards as upheld and expressed by undergraduate grades is that they forecast achievement beyond the precincts of the college. Representing the attainment of various forms of intellectual skill, they predict success in those sectors of what even academicians call "the real world," to which such capabilities supposedly generalize widely. Unhappily, systematic investigations of this plausible and attractive contention yield consistently negative results. In literally forty-nine out of fifty studies, the correlation of undergraduate grades to indices of postgraduate success is insignificant. The same outcome seems to occur regardless of the criterion of extracollegiate achievement—the amount of earned annual income, listing in directories of the eminent, like *Who's Who* or *American Men of Science,* ratings by supervisors of teaching performance in public schools, evaluations by corporations of their junior executives, number or judged impact of published works, rate and level of promotion in business or governmental organizations, and so forth.

Two exceptions are on the record. One is the rapidity of promotion in a national public utility in which the individual's complete dossier, including his college transcript, is reviewed like a Navy "jacket" each time a promotion period comes around. Apparently because high college grades impart a kind of continuing mark of prestige to the set of papers considered, they are significantly related to success in this one large firm. Statistical purists are likely to be troubled by the extent to which the predictor contaminates the criterion in this situation; from the massive drift of the evidence, all of us must at least entertain the possibility that the company's procedures rather than the inherent character of college grades account for the results. The second exception is the obvious one: undergraduate grades do indeed significantly forecast grades in graduate school—an unsurprising finding that nevertheless raises the faintly upsetting issue of whether many of us who have spent some large part of our careers as graduate faculty members and as makers of Ph.D.s have really been doing much that differs fundamentally from the labors of our colleagues in undergraduate vineyards. Commonalities here could be troubling in the light of the university's traditional insistence on differences—differences in such rewards as salary and status, in the investment of institutional resources, in conditions of work like teaching load, and in other important factors of institutional life. Pleasantly, however, these matters need not, in this context, concern us long.

What must concern us are the implications of our systematic observations so far, plus one additional (and familiar) datum. Undergraduate grades seem to lack a significant relationship to indices of post-baccalaureate success; they are significantly correlated with grades in graduate school, and—our additional bit of information—they are significantly *inter*correlated. As a matter of fact, the strongest relationships of undergraduate grades are to each other. We can clarify the point in two ways: first, students who earn As (or Ds) in Spanish are, *mirabile dictu,* more likely to earn As (or Ds) in mathematics than they are to succeed (or do badly) in the consular service or the export business. Put another way, grades in Spanish predict grades in calculus more effectively than they discriminate the winners from the losers in jobs to which Spanish fluency may be relevant. There is nothing special, of course, about Spanish and mathematics here; we could just as well refer to psychology and literary studies or chemistry and economics. When all of our oxen are gored, none of us need be defensive.

But we are. And we are, at least in part, because these findings badly ripple the waters of our faith in academic standards as the foundation of the opportunity that a college education defines. The student who capitalizes best on that opportunity is the one who wins our most favorable judgments on our terms, for he is now the best equipped to deal with the world outside our halls. The question before us is one of whether such is really the case. Although, as Kuhn and others have wryly emphasized, facts rarely alter the structures of our beliefs, the facts that we have reviewed suggest an alternative interpretation. That interpretation splits into two quite distinctive parts.

First, in a perhaps loose but yet reasonably well understood fashion, the term *academic standards* refers to the judgments and expectancies that the professional members of the university community hold in relation to one another. What the term specifies are the canons of value among scholars practicing their specialized arts. In this sense, the idea of academic standards has great legitimacy and usefulness, reflecting the academic mores with respect to the essentially symbolic competencies that are properly central to the historically defined disciplines. There is clearly nothing to denigrate here and much to honor. These norms of intellectual effort have accumulated through the last century, if not through the last seven hundred years, more than enough evidence of their merit to command both respect and gratitude. Universities, in serving frequently as great engines of research and fountains of insightful cultural criticism, occupy a unique and positive place among America's social institutions. In many respects, that place has been won and preserved by virtue—the word has almost its old French connotations—of the passionate seriousness that our professoriate has invested in the standards of its crafts and in the conditions essential to their exercise.

Difficulties arise in connection with my second point: When these professional conceptions of academic standards are applied *edu-*

cationally and transformed into such devices as undergraduate grades, they tend to define a closed and limited system of a subtle and significant sort. Successful students become those whose skills, values, and behavior most closely approximate those of their mentors. A bit more jargonistically, we can make the case this way: our best students are the ones who most fully accept us as role-models. The keys to the restricted range of roles that those standards specify are primarily the symbolic skills and the specialized forms of technical knowledge that are the common currency of the disciplines. Remembering that these skills and these kinds of cognitive achievements are most intimately related internally—that is, to each other—rather than to some external, extracollegiate criterion, it is at least challenging also to recall three features of our distinctive, if not unique, academic landscape. First, whenever the economic circumstances of our institutions permit, we *select* those students, who, at the time of admission, give evidence of high symbolic ability and considerable informational mastery. Second, our *scheme of examinations* concentrates almost exclusively on these same dimensions of proficiency. Self-awareness, interpersonal and intercultural competence, organizational talent, and the several varieties of creativity may have won some lip-service from us in recent years, but they have yet to show up in our testing procedures in any extensive way. Third, our undergraduate *reward system* of grade-point averages, such honors as election to Phi Beta Kappa or *summa cum laude* graduation, and even personal access—the friendliness allowed or encouraged between student and professor—is geared to the same conceptions of upper-level proficiency. Once again, there is no basis for denigration here; in the contemporary world, symbolic capabilities and technical knowledge need no defense. But the closed system of the academy has proved difficult to open, in spite of genuine good will and large-scale effort, in any broadly useful fashion to America's historically disenfranchised minorities and its white lower class. The relatively narrow standards of proficiency that essentially identify that system fit only loosely and uncomfortably the conditions of pluralism, where exploration and personal goal-setting, individual development, and growth in the capacity to make informed and cool-headed decisions in the face of changing circumstances seem more suitable, as well as being increasingly in demand.

If, however, the academic system is a closed one, we are brought almost to the brink of paradox when we face its relationship to the function of sorting and certifying that our society has imposed upon its colleges and universities. How can so self-contained an arrangement fulfill so external a requirement? That issue may be resolved in some helpful measure by examining some of the traditional concomitants of role-acceptance among undergraduates. If students were expected to perform according to standards of symbolic competence and disciplinary achievement, they were also expected to shape their behavior to fit the contours of less intellectual mores. Although it comes always as a slight shock to the marginal men that many of us professors are, the fact remains that faculty members and academic administrators have been conventionally viewed as representatives of the dominant middle class, and the notion of the scholar-*gentleman* implies values and qualities of conduct that reach beyond the boundaries of cognition and technical expertise. In times when both social stability and social mobility took middle-class membership as their targets of choice, and when middleclass manners and a middle-class identity were prerequisites to a firmer footing on the ladder of social esteem and economic advancement, these tangential standards of college life had a special importance. Along with the character-building process of hard academic work, they supplied the commitments and the personal polish of socialization. Policies of *in loco parentis* reinforced and extended this complicated and only partially articulate function of higher education. As a consequence of this function, exercised partly by selection and partly by primarily indirect tuition, undergraduate institutions have in significant degree sorted and certified people less for particular and specialized occupational roles than for more generalized social ones. The baccalaureate degree, in a quiet but forceful fashion, represents, whatever else it may signify, a person who has demonstrated his ability and his willingness to act in accordance with middle-class norms.

This conception of things suggests nothing trivial. The corporate and governmental organizations of the modern world are largely founded on middle-class virtues and middle-class values. Such virtues and values are intimately associated with the elites that supply much of that world's leadership, and the rewards of social recognition and economic benefit have been mainly distributed through the changing, somewhat amorphous, but always recognizable middle class. So long as the myths of a dynamically open class system and of the melting pot retained their vitality, the hegemony of the middle class and the image of the WASP as the prototype of the successful American only occasionally faced strong challenges.

During the last decade, however, as those myths became eroded and as American consciousness changed under the impact of Vietnam, of the overdue insistence on their own cultural integrity by our racial minorities, of a growing awareness of the distressing conflict between environmental quality and highly technologized forms of economic growth, and of the stressful pace and massiveness of social change, our shared faith appears to have undergone a sea-change. Is the backbone of our society *really* a middle class, enduringly wise and unshakeably reliable, forged and reforged through processes of cultural assimilation? Doubts nag our minds and chivvy our feelings. In the anxiety spawned by doubt, many of us react by roaring our reaffirmation, following the old practice of substituting volume for conviction under conditions of unease. If such a substitution may be a significant element in our current politics, it may figure, too, in our educational policies. The preservation of academic standards *as we have historically known them* may relieve our discomfort by raising a bastion against the enormously difficult problems with which the entailments of pluralism threaten to flood us. Apart from the questions of whether that bastion is illusory or real, and of what it may cost in social utility and in painful contradictions of traditional American ideals, our current situation has occasioned, it seems, a curiously inverted instance of culture lag.

Most of us associated with the academy ordinarily think of ourselves as in the vanguard of society, perceiving first, if only dimly, the shapes of things to come. When we trouble the larger culture of which we are inextricably a part, it is because we confront it with the novelties in criticism, in ideas, and in technical perspectives and inventions to which it must eventually accommodate. At the moment, not only is public mistrust of higher education at an all-time high, but other social institutions, for all their stumbling, appear to be grappling more effectively with the issues of pluralism. In spite of Wounded Knee and the summary closing down of the Office of Economic Opportunity and related federal agencies and programs, the courts, social agencies and community organizations, some of the professions and some segments of industry, a number of large voluntary associations, and a significant few state and local governments have taken striking steps in two directions. One is toward the launching of educational efforts that involve either a diversity of people or a traditionally neglected group, and that focus on such transdisciplinary problems and interests as the determination of alternative futures, or the conception and de-

velopment of novel sex roles, or the processes of interracial cooperation in communities. The other explores ways of incorporating conventionally underrepresented persons into occupations and into social
roles without requiring them to lose their cultural identity. From the
point of view of many, these moves have been sporadic, slow, and
marked by high costs in both interpersonal conflicts and inefficiency.
Yet it is at least arguable that their accomplishments in coping with
pluralistic social forces have exceeded those of the university and that
the successes registered and the expectancies aroused in those extra-
academic arenas define the sources from which the pressures of pluralism have been brought to bear on the halls of higher learning. The
converse of this reading of things may be less controversial: One looks
in vain for telling evidence that the university has *generated* much of
the impetus to pluralism or that it has adjusted its undergraduate standards in order to provide educational opportunities that serve the concerns of a pluralistic world. The reasons for the lag may be persuasive
ones although they will not be free from dissent. The compelling question here is one of whether the lag itself, if it does in fact exist, does
not represent a strange and disturbing turn in the relationship of the
university to its society.

When we shift from the nature of our inherited and prevalent
academic standards to their relationship to academicians, we find little
grounds for surprise. The data are available from both direct experience and from studies that run from Logan Wilson's *Academic Man*
of 1942 through the more recent investigations by Brown, Gross and
Grambsch, and others. Most of us as professors and administrators
either derive from or have won a place in the middle class. The route
that we have followed has taken us through intensive training in one
of the academic professions; and our pride, directed largely by the
socialization process of which the Ph.D. is the culmination, rests heavily on our performance as technical scholars, whether our discipline be
literary study or chemistry. We place high value on "brightness," which
means adeptness in the manipulation of verbal and quantitative symbols, and we commit ourselves with few qualifications to the representation and advancement of the research-oriented fields of inquiry in
which we find our identity. Our contribution to the ever-expanding
sum of technical and professional knowledge has been prodigious.

Tension arises from the societal assumption that the education
of young people consists basically of their exposure to these practition-
ers of professional scholarship. That assumption, which casts technical

investigators in the role of undergraduate teachers, has enjoyed a kind of empirical validation for almost a century, despite two quite different indicators of turbulence under the calm surface of its success. One of these indicators is the academic novel. From Owen Wister's *Philosophy 4* to Nicholas von Hoffman's *Two, Three, Many More,* that odd genre, usually produced by college graduates with the most pleasing academic records, has testified consistently to student dissatisfaction and disappointment with the undergraduate experience. Indeed, one is hard-pressed to find a single instance of the fictional portrayal of college life that presents it in positive terms. Substantively, the second indicator, the large body of research on student evaluations of the processes of higher education, confirms systematically the judgments suggested by the academic novel. The learnings considered most significant by students, for example, either while they are still undergraduates or as much as five years beyond the baccalaureate degree, are consistently those that occur outside classroom settings. When graduates are asked from five to ten years after leaving college to identify the faculty members who had a major impact on their lives and thinking, they remember, on the average, slightly less than two names. And the literature is discouragingly extensive and consistent on the large differences between the perceptions of academic professionals of the purposes of colleges and universities and the perceptions of students of those purposes.

These tensions find still further expression in the finding by Talcott Parsons and Gerald Platt that the primary motivation for undergraduate teaching by professors in universities is the recruitment of bright youngsters to one's own discipline. A kind of messianic component in the academic impulse seems to operate here: Symbolically capable students with a taste for conceptual complexity and the mastery of intellectual information must be saved from the Mordor of majoring in history or physics to enjoy the Rivendell of literary scholarship or psychology. In any event, the professorial emphasis is on the transmission of professional expertness and the content and methods of technical fields of scholarship. If there is much to praise here and much to be socially grateful for, there is also a marked contrast between this notion of the educative function of colleges and universities and such notions as the facilitation of student-directed learning, or the informed exploration of personal potentials, or the cultivation of a wider range of talents than the professional skills to which the academy has almost exclusively given a home. It is important to realize that the vagueness in these alternatives tends to be more irritatingly obvious to those of us who hold membership in the academic professions than to the students in their pluralistic diversity who now make demands upon our ivied halls.

In this setting, I want to consider the relationship of academic standards to one of the major aspects of our institutional dynamics. Every college or university offers, in effect, to each of its potential undergraduates an agreement which he must accept. As a kind of summary prototype, the customary form of that agreement can be stated more or less in these terms:

"As an institution of higher learning, we will admit you for two reasons: We have a certificate (and a wealth of knowledge to support it) that you want and need, and you have the symbolic abilities that lead us to believe that you will be a credit to us. You may remain with us, however, only so long as you meet our academic standards; and if you want the certificate called a baccalaureate degree, then you must follow the sequence of studies that we prescribe."

There is a brand of justice in this formulation, and its legitimacy is enhanced by long familiarity. It poses a problem, however, in relation to our growing interest in more pluralistic responsibilities. For ghetto applicants, and for others for whom college was not available until quite recently, this kind of agreement virtually guarantees wholesale failure. If previously inadmissible students are accepted as a matter of social rather than educational policy, if they are required to take our current courses, and if they are subjected to our present academic standards, then, as experience has already demonstrated, large numbers of them simply do not (literally) make the grade. The familiar image of the open door becoming the revolving door is cruelly apt here. If, on the other hand, academic opportunity for these students is defined by deliberately diluted courses or by remedial work that provides little or no college-level credit, then humiliation and unfair expense in time and somebody's money are the unfortunate entailments. Not so parenthetically, it is well to remind ourselves that declining enrollments reflect in some small but significant part a shared, if not entirely articulate, longing by relatively advantaged white middle-class students for wider educational options.

That first and traditional agreement contrasts markedly with another specification of the contractual relationship between an undergraduate enterprise and its students. This alternative, only one of several that our imaginations can reach, might be phrased like this:

"Everyone who is interested in what we have to offer—recognizing that what we have to offer is far from infinite—is invited so long as we have room. You will be expected to identify what you want most to learn and how you want to develop. You will have to negotiate your own standards of success in meeting the goals that you set, and your remaining here as a student depends on (a) your working hard on the achievement of your self-determined objectives and (b) your functioning as a positively contributory member of our community. We will try to provide a range of experiences from which you can choose as you go about your business of exploration and development, and we have some people here who will try to help you so long as you convince them of your seriousness. For as long as you find yourself able to capitalize on the opportunities that we furnish and on the abilities of the people that we have available, we hope that you will stay with us."

This statement is not without its implication of standards. It values hard work and seriousness; it recognizes the limitations under which any institution must labor, and it specifies the basic grounds for retention and expulsion. Neither softness nor sentimentality is inherent in it. But it recognizes diversity; it represents an attempt to harness educational procedures to a larger awareness of both social justice and human talent, and it puts a greater premium on learning and personal development than on the transmission of disciplinary competence.

Any reaching in such a direction entails Herculean effort and some downright agony to make success probable. But unless at least some institutions begin to search along such lines and to think seriously about the educational services that such orientations imply, the present clash between pluralism and academic standards, both of which lie so clearly in the realm of human goods, does indeed define the groundwork for tragedy—a tragedy that none of us wants either to attend or to participate in.

PART FIVE

Postsecondary Education: The New Perimeters

✁✁✁✁✁✁✁✁✁✁✁✁✁✁

During the last quarter century, there has been a great shift in national goals for higher education in the United States. In President Truman's administration, official federal policy did not neglect vocational training, but it strongly favored the development of what was then called "general education." At that time there was almost universal agreement among educators, as America prepared itself to become The Great Society, that an education for the future must emphasize problem-solving techniques in various fields of knowledge, must stress the abilities that a person needs when he meets new situations, must inculcate attitudes that are appropriate to a world of change, and must train students in the skills of observation, analysis, and communication—all regardless of what specific job the student would en-

ter when he graduated from college. Studies during that period showed that well over half of our college graduates eventually ended up in careers that were not related to their majors in college. There seemed to be all the more reason, then, for supporting the goals of liberal education and for stressing problem-solving abilities that would be applicable to a large number of different sorts of jobs.

In recent years, however, educational aims throughout the nation have narrowed. Accompanying the stress on equality of educational opportunity, vocational and semiprofessional objectives have been receiving increased emphasis, and federal policies have clearly favored what is now called "career education." These new emphases in educational objectives, and new forms of financial aid to carry them out, are reflected in significant recent national legislation affecting our profession—namely, the Education Amendments of 1972. The essays of Part Five are concerned with various aspects of this legislation, analyzing its implications for future developments in the entire postsecondary field.

The nature of this closing section of the yearbook is appropriate to the overall design of the volume. Starting with the concrete political and economic emphases of Parts One and Two, we moved in the essays of Parts Three and Four to an entirely different level of thinking—a level that deals with the long-range problems of the future of our civilization and the function of its colleges and universities. With Part Five, we return to the present and to the more immediate future.

The authors of the four essays—Jack H. Jones, George P. Doherty, Joseph P. Cosand, and Roger W. Heyns—bring us back to today and turn our minds toward the decisions that will affect us tomorrow. They show us clearly how much larger and more complex will be the new world of "postsecondary" education than has been the world of "higher" education to which we have long been accustomed.

The message in all of this is neatly summed up by Roger Heyns in the essay which closes the volume: "In our newly awakened concern for the nontraditional, the vocational, and the technical, and for the proprietary institutions, we must not now demean the absolutely essential activities of the large research or graduate institutions. They, in turn, must not in their current embattled state derogate the newly enfranchised. And all the other types [of educational institutions] must develop those same feelings of mutual respect."

JOSEPH AXELROD

19

Proprietary Schools as a National Resource

Jack H. Jones

The Education Amendments of 1972 have given greater recognition to the proprietary school than any previous legislation. In the Amendments, Congress defined a Proprietary Institution of Higher Education as one that is accredited. Accreditation is the important factor; there is no exception. Further, the definition requires that the school offer educational programs of not less than six months in length. Proprietary schools are accredited by four accrediting agencies recognized by the U.S. Commissioner of Education, after meeting criteria published by him in the Federal Register, and have the force and effect of law. The same criteria are applicable to regional associations as well as other nationally recognized accrediting agencies. The four agencies are the Association of Independent Colleges and Schools, formerly the Accrediting Commission for Business Schools, the National Association of Trade and Technical Schools, the National Home Study Council, and an Accrediting Commission for Cosmetology Schools. These agencies were founded and are sustained without any federal or foundation funds.

The jurisdiction of these agencies is not limited to proprietary schools. The Association of Independent Colleges and Schools accredits proprietary schools as well as nonprofit institutions. The Commission also accredits business schools at the collegiate level as well as at the vocational level. The institution of which I am president, Jones College, is an example. The college has been a recognized nonprofit organization since 1947. It is accredited as a four-year senior college of business, with authority to grant associate and bachelor of science degrees.

Although it has been estimated that there are about ten thousand proprietary vocational schools in the country, the Education Amendments do not affect a large number. There are probably about twelve hundred business schools, thirty-five hundred trade or technical schools, and a like number of beauty and barber schools, with the remainder made up of other specialized schools. The Amendments affect only accredited schools with programs of six months or more. This eliminates a large number of proprietary schools. I estimate the total number of accredited proprietary schools at less than fifteen hundred.

There is probably general agreement that the backbone of any institution is its students, and that in our struggle for survival we have built into the system a form of competitiveness between educational institutions which has manifested itself in programs designed to attract students. Historically, proprietary school students have had no access to federal money. It was therefore necessary for them to become highly receptive to new programs to draw students. Moreover, once students enter, it was important to keep them motivated to continue and complete their studies. The rate of retention of students to completion of the course of study is very high in these schools, even though they compete for students with institutions charging little or no tuition.

Proprietary education has been, and is, incorrectly conceptualized as offering a particular type of educational program, or a particular level of complexity of vocational offerings. In my view, however, proprietary education is merely one form of institutional governance; there are taxpaying institutions; there are tax-avoiding institutions; and there are tax-consuming institutions. The proprietary school must not only pay taxes, but it must sustain itself on tuition income. Such schools must start from a different premise. Proprietary education starts like the recipe for a rabbit stew—first you catch the rabbit. The proprietary school must be a student-oriented school; student primacy must be the principal objective.

Such schools, by and large, do not have, and are not comfortable with, research facilities or research people. They are not conceptualizers; they have a very simple, goal-oriented way of training people for jobs. And inasmuch as the proprietary school must sustain itself on tuition income, the role of its chief administrative officer is quite different from that of the typical college president. He devotes no time to fund-raising or other such duties usual to the college president, but engages in other activities, the main thrust of which is the student body. He works closely with his director of education to provide courses and schedules designed to accommodate the wants, needs, and convenience of the students, and these considerations take precedence over those for the faculty, staff, and administration. It is his philosophy that his is an institution of specialization, and that the students are there to learn, the teachers to teach, and administrators to administer.

The recruiting efforts of proprietary schools are not directed toward the student who wants to attend college while "finding himself," rather it seeks the student who has decided upon a career goal, who is impatient to get started, who is determined to earn the right to the "good life," and who is enthusiastic about his future. To serve such students the school does not offer an educational smorgasbord, but provides specialized programs and courses designed to prepare the student to qualify for his career objective in the shortest possible time. As the result of a streamlined curriculum, the faculty load is greater, but preparation time is less than in the traditional institutions. There is light emphasis on sports and other extracurricular activities, but heavy emphasis on preparation for career success.

Among accredited colleges in the country, about 10 percent of the nonprofit colleges are not accredited. For the proprietary institutions in the post-secondary field, however, the figures are reversed. Only about 10 to 15 percent are accredited. From a public relations point of view, the good schools are categorized with the bad. Proprietary education is still handicapped, like any minority group, because its lowest common denominator determines its image—twice as much effort may produce about half as much recognition. This situation was nicely illustrated for me in a conversation with the president of a college in Florida. I was telling him about the Katherine Gibbs School in New York, and his reaction was: "That's such a good school, I had no idea that it was proprietary!"

Acceptance of the proprietary schools by the educational establishment has been long denied. But the statutory definitions and policy pronouncements by the Congress in the Amendments of 1972 signal a growing recognition of the place of these institutions in the academic turf. One of the key policy pronouncements by the Congress in the Amendments was the establishment of the state commissions mandated by Section 1202. This new policy of the Congress, whether or not it is implemented by appropriations in fiscal 1974, may have a greater impact on the future of proprietary schools than any other federal legislation of the past ten years. The state commissions were designed to coordinate the planning of post-secondary education within the states with respect to the utilization of federal funds for such purposes. The Amendments provide that these commissions be broadly and equitably representative of "the general public, and public and private nonprofit and proprietary institutions of post-secondary education in the State." Although it is a major disappointment that the federal budget for fiscal 1974 has failed to provide for the implementation of these committees, and they may not be activated, at least for the present, the recognition of the proprietary school is established as congressional policy.

Another important gain for the proprietary sector is the full eligibility of their students for all forms of federal student financial aid—eligibility for whatever money is appropriated. Concern about the lack of appropriations is not as great among proprietary institutions as it is among other institutions in higher education because they know they can operate successfully without these aids. But they *are* concerned because they are a part of the educational community and they sincerely hope these serious problems can be solved. Proprietary schools have never been eligible, and are not now eligible, for the categorical and institutional aid programs. They were never dependent upon them in the first place. Further, they have never had any expectation whatsoever of participation, because their declared philosophy was that they were only interested in seeing that their students were eligible for aid. These schools have never asked, and in my opinion will never ask, for any type of institutional aid.

As they see the general principles of the Amendments of 1972, proprietary institutions gain thereby a new sense of responsibility, a new opportunity to serve, and a new challenge. Indeed, it is somewhat ironic that as proprietary schools seek to conform to the collegiate norms of yesteryear, the norms are being abandoned by the colleges themselves. As proprietary schools achieve specific authority to confer college degrees, the desire of college students for such credentials seems to be displaced by their desire to achieve competence. Proprietary education has long been a hardy weed in the academic grove. It has survived, and at times prospered, because it has lived with the realities of its own pretentions. When the proprietary school abandons its heritage of flexibility and specialized service and attempts to act and operate like the rest of the educational establishment, it abandons its heritage and encourages its own extinction.

For proprietary education, the years immediately ahead should be good ones. Student aspirations, fiscal realities, and changing national goals, indicate that the right of proprietary institutions to exist is no longer challenged. Rather, they are recognized as a legitimate national resource, and are encouraged to make available their services. Hence the opportunity and the responsibility is now theirs. The years ahead will show whether their capacity to respond creatively and realistically to that responsibility matches their present opportunity.

20

Case Study: The Bell and Howell Schools

George P. Doherty

☙☙☙☙☙☙☙☙☙☙☙☙

Not very much is known, generally, by people in higher education about Bell and Howell Schools. I shall therefore devote a few lines to describing both the resident and home-study schools so that the rest of what I have to say can be more easily evaluated.

We have eleven thousand students in residence on eight campuses, seven of which are in the United States and one which is in Canada. Six operate under the name of the DeVry Institute of Technology, one is the Ohio Institute of Technology, and one the Central Institute of Technology. About half the students work toward an accredited degree (associate's or bachelor's) in electronics engineering technology, over a period of nine or twelve quarters. The other half spend six quarters studying to become electronics technicians. The six-quarter course teaches little theory, except by derivation, and no formal math beyond arithmetic. The bachelor's degree program is made up of roughly three-fifths electronics engineering technology, one-fifth physics and mathematics, one-tenth English, communications, and humanities courses, and one-tenth economics, management, and other business administration courses. Throughout the program, our students' schedules uniformly call for twenty-five hours of class of which six are laboratory hours.

Accreditation of the degree courses is by the Engineers' Council for Professional Development. In a few of the newer schools, the curriculum leading to a bachelor's degree has not existed long enough to achieve such accreditation; presently, the students are candidates for the degree. The schools generally are accredited by the National Association of Trade and Technical Schools.

In addition to the resident students, we have about one hundred thousand active students studying at home to become electronics technicians. These students do lessons and lab exercises on equipment supplied by us. Also, each working day two thousand of these students-at-home telephone us, free, on our WATS lines, for help and consultation. In the course of a year, about twenty-five thousand students (25 percent of all active home students) voluntarily attend monthly Saturday classes held in over fifty cities throughout the United States and Canada; such attendance is increasing sharply and will soon become mandatory on a basis yet to be determined. Our electronics home-study students can transfer into the resident school six-quarter technician program with full credit, and many are doing so. Many of the principles of the open university are already in practice in our home-study schools. We are rapidly becoming a full-fledged "open institute."

Finally, we also have over twenty-five thousand home-study students in accounting in the same kind of program, and with the same relative participation in telephone calls and monthly classes. Both accounting and electronics programs are accredited by the National Home Study Council. In our degree programs we have a completely "open admissions" policy, requiring only a high school diploma or G.E.D. certificate. For our other programs, we have no entrance requirements, but in electronics we exclude persons with certain physical defects that prevent employment.

Our primary goal in education is optimum employability of the graduate throughout his lifetime, to the extent that education can achieve it. This means that each graduate must be fully equipped for, and competent in, the current *and* the developing state of the art when he or she graduates. In the case of degree graduates, who have studied longer and acquired theoretical knowledge and an ability to reason mathematically (and otherwise) to solve problems, it means also that we must enhance their ability to grow and change with the state of the art throughout their working lives. They can command salaries significantly higher than the technicians can.

A second major goal is that our students become more civilized human beings. We think this improves employability, but, whether it does or not, it is an important goal. The means to this end, in the case of our graduates, cannot be prior, formal, liberal arts education. I wish it could—my son is in such a program at Macalester College, and I am the product of one—but our students have not the means to pursue this as preparation for career education, and their previous education has given them little or no desire for it. Therefore, to achieve this second goal, we concentrate on improving their communications skills, broadly defined to include listening to other people and perceiving their concerns. Also, we think that the ability to reason well and to solve problems implies intellectual curiosity, and often also creativity, and when we implant and foster those qualities, we tend to civilize.

You can see, I hope, that our goal is not at all to supply mindless technician-servants for a mindless technological society. I suggest that if most of the graduates of postsecondary education were servant technicians, civilization would face a bleak future. We are committed to the motto of New York State University, "Let each become all he is capable of being."

Bell and Howell Schools are a small part—something under 5 percent—of the world of proprietary education. It would be presumptuous of me to appear here as the representative of proprietary education. Proprietary education is the very opposite of monolithic. If there is a general tendency in proprietary education, I suspect it is to provide short courses of several months, aimed at supplying competence in the *current* state of an art or craft. There is absolutely nothing wrong with this, provided that the course is fully current and assures employability. Unfortunately, many proprietary school graduates are not readily employable—I would not guess at the percentage—but, of course, that is also true in non-proprietary education. The fault here is only partly with the postsecondary schools. Much of it relates to the poor quality of the students' prior education.

One other thing needs to be said about proprietary education in general. In the past, and with good reason, there has been much concern about dishonest or high-pressure selling by business-owned schools. Many such schools existed by selling enrollment contracts to unsophisticated people, delivering little or nothing of value, and collecting as much money as possible on the contracts. Recent legislation has reduced this problem to a small-scale one, particularly the Federal Trade Commission guidelines respecting selling and advertising, and the contract refund requirements by states, accrediting agencies, and the Veterans Administration.

I will refer often here to the experience of Bell and Howell Schools, because I can be more concrete and more accurate about our goals, our degree of success, our concerns, and our problems than I could be if I were to generalize about proprietary education. This may make clear the differences between us and traditional education, and the similarities, too.

It seems to us that the single question of overriding importance that all of us, including the nonprofit schools, have failed to deal with, and *continue* to fail to deal with, is, what should our graduates be? Even in career education, the question of what a graduate should be tends to be answered, by us and by others, academically and theoretically, rather than empirically. And the objective, and the program to achieve it, lag the state of the career art by intervals which are unnecessarily, inexcusably long—intervals which reflect the ivory tower isolation of the school curriculum developers, both proprietary and nonproprietary. Advisory committees are only a minor part of the solution. To deal with this problem, which is to say to determine objectives as precisely and realistically as possible, there needs to be continuous research *in the field*, in plants, R and D laboratories, and business offices, involving incessant interchange between educators, on the one hand, and engineering managers and managers of business, on the other.

We think we need very creative, imaginative, and, of course, fully competent educators to spend all their time in such field research in order to answer the question, what should the graduate be? We are developing such men, including an experienced, successful, engineering manager who directs them, at the top level of the managment of our schools. It seems significant that finding men who have had any experience of this kind is a needle-in-a-haystack problem.

One reason that this way of defining what the gradaute should be is so important is that, with a very few exceptions among giant companies (General Motors and IBM are examples) employers are not prepared to finish the incomplete education of graduates who are not up to the state of the art or who have such basic deficiencies as having had no experience in problem-solving or operating as members of project teams, and so on. Employers' training capabilities are, on the whole, pitifully inadequate. They are and, I suppose, must be limited to adapting the graduate to the employer's specific, local, individual needs and environment. I suspect this is unlikely to change, partly because of employee turnover, and partly because employers are not educators.

Moreover, the graduate should not be defined solely in terms of his immediate market value at the time of graduation. We work for the student and future graduate, and not, except incidentally, for his future employer. Therefore, we must prepare him to adapt to a rapidly changing world so that he can limit and reduce his own personal rate of obsolescence. Solving this problem is, of course, easier said than done; in my opinion it relates directly to our success in enhancing creative and problem-solving abilities, and in teaching awareness of the self as responsible for the exercise of career options, for complete self-protection in place of reliance on company or institutional father figures. It also relates to informing the student thoroughly about the larger system or environment in which he will work, the structure and dynamics of the typical business, and the various kinds of roles that people in his career field can and do play.

Assume that we define the graduate well—better than, in my opinion, any of us are now doing. The single most difficult problem of most schools, especially those with open admissions policies, seems quite clear: how to accept people who vary enormously in arithmetic and verbal skills and bring them, in two to four academic years, to the level of the graduate. This implies a large-scale remedial effort to enable as many students as possible to achieve the starting requirements. Between 35 and 40 percent of all entering students undergo remedial education. We test all entering resident students regardless of their high school performance, and we counsel them; then we place them in one of three groups, depending mainly on their skill with numbers. If the tests prove to have been false indicators, the students are quickly transferred. A student may have as much as two quarters of remedial education prior to the time he enters the degree program. Some of these students who could enter the degree program don't want to; a greater number simply cannot be brought up to the required level of arithmetic competence in two quarters, and they enter the six-quarter technician program or drop out. This is a weakness in our program; if we could extend our remedial effort beyond two quarters, we could rescue many more students. We are exploring ways to accomplish this.

Before we established our open admissions policy, relatively few students dropped out after the second quarter of the regular, resident (campus) curriculum, and about 50 percent of the entering students graduated. This percentage continues to apply to the group of students who enter the regular curriculum, without remedial instruction. Of the students who enter school at the remedial level, 30–35 percent graduate from the regular curriculum. When we began our remedial program early in 1971, this percentage was lower; recently it has been exhibiting a strong, steady increase. Twenty-five percent of our students are black, and the attrition percentages for black students are not significantly different from those for whites. An important factor in our program to enable students to achieve the level of ability of the graduate has always been that our students are scheduled in class and lab twenty-five hours per week.

Tuition for Bell and Howell Schools is $586 in the first quarter; thereafter it is $456 per quarter. It has been at these rates for two years, allowing us to operate at a modest profit. Since our students are from families struggling to pay their current living expenses, we must finance tuition for more than half our students until they graduate and begin their careers. We must also obtain parttime jobs, averaging twenty hours per week for 75 percent of them, at the highest possible wage per hour, and we must help them obtain the best possible housing for the dollars they spend.

We are proud of our faculties. In the degree program, they hold masters and bachelors' degrees in engineering, science, technology, and the humanities. In the technician program, they tend to be chiefly men of industrial experience, and we do not require degrees. Company policy provides for full reimbursement for tuition if they take additional course work themselves. All faculty members spend all their time teaching and counseling; they do no outside research and publish almost nothing. The devotion our faculties have to their students is, in my mind, little less than saintly.

These are our goals, our principles, our philosophy, if you like. Our achievement is imperfect, but rapidly improving. One test of that is that 90 percent of our graduates get career jobs within sixty days, many with our help. (About 5 percent of our graduates will not move from their home towns. This imposes a limitation which, at least temporarily, may prevent their employment in the career for which we educated them.)

Not once in five years of operation of our schools has the funding of any program been reduced because of profit considerations. We spend what must be spent to accomplish our quality objectives, but we avoid unnecessary high costs, and fiscal soundness results. Of course this is not just because we are good managers. We *are* frugal, as *The Chronicle of Higher Education* recently said, but our specialization also helps enormously in controlling costs. A restaurant serving fifty entrees will only survive with an enormous trade and high prices; unhappily this principle applies also to schools.

Proprietary education is no different from non-proprietary education in that both are faced with costs rising faster than the economy as a whole, simply because both, like medical care, are almost wholly labor-intensive. But, unlike medical care with its company- and institutionally-subsidized insurance and Medicare, education has very uncertain sources of funds to ease this problem, either by supplementing tuition or by financing students until they can repay the loans out of the career earnings which result from their education. Obviously, there is no satisfactory present answer to this problem. I simply want to note that proprietary education has ways of dealing with the control of costs which differ greatly from public and tax-supported private education. I think there may be profit in exploring these differences. This is not a matter of business looking down its nose at non-business. It is an observation that techniques differ greatly. From month-to-month, business managers are required to forecast actual results compared with budget, to compare standard unit costs with actual unit costs, and to justify variations. The penalties for failure to fulfill financial commitments, within time and money limits, are severe. This can be a very positive thing provided that the adjustments made do not cut quality and service standards. When some businesses and some proprietary schools do cut too far it is self-defeating because it kills demand.

I do not think that any harm can result from comparing financial control techniques. None of us has a nickel to waste. Few proprietary schools and few businesses of any kind use cost-benefit analysis effectively in decision-making. This technique, developed by the Rand Corporation, used by McNamara in the Pentagon with varying success, and generally neglected since, is, in my opinion, the most powerful analytical tool we have for fiscal purposes, and one that can be much more useful than it is today to all post-secondary schools.

Socrates said, "The unexamined life is not worth living." Very few businesses, and few proprietary schools, reexamine what they are doing in any way except superficially and peripherally. That is why so few businesses are flexible enough to adjust to change. I believe this to be true of postsecondary education, too.

21

Implementing the Education Amendments of 1972

Joseph P. Cosand

The Education Amendments of 1972, three years in the making, absorbing the time and energy of untold numbers of educators, lay persons, organizational representatives, state legislators, and congressional representatives and senators, were finally approved in the summer of 1972, but only after long and bitter argument in the Conference Committee. In general, most of those involved believed that the Amendments represented a great achievement for higher education, and among many individuals and groups, the legislation became known as the Higher Education Bill in 1972. This was a misnomer, but it did indicate the importance of the legislation to the higher education community.

Following the approval by Congress and the President, actions were initiated by the federal government, by states, by organizations, by individual institutions, and by groups representing the above, to clarify the legislation—to reach agreement on the intent of Congress, and to develop Issue Papers of Rules, Regulations, and Guidelines which would enable the legislation to be implemented when funded.

There was confusion, especially because of disagreement concerning the interpretation of the wording of the legislation with respect to Congressional intent. At the same time there was an eagerness on the part of most of those involved to get on with the action, for the scope of the Amendments was unmatched in history. This was indeed an historical occasion—a revolution in higher education—a time of excitement for students and institutions alike. Students were to be provided with an entitlement; equality of opportunity was to become a reality—not just a dream. Institutions for the first time in history were to be provided general institutional aid whether they were public or private. Proprietary institutions were to be included under the umbrella of federal assistance, and higher education was to become known as postsecondary education—a broader base to serve a broader student population. State Planning Commissions were to be established, with federal assistance, to bring postsecondary education together in order to do a better job with respect to quality, efficiency, and use of resources, both human and material, to make a reality out of equality of opportunity and equal access—access for whom, to what, and for what purpose?

There were many other sections of the Amendments which offered encouragement and anticipation to students and institutions, and, of even greater importance, to society as a whole. Community colleges were to be expanded in order that most of our population would have access to a postsecondary institution within commuting distance. Occupational education was to be emphasized so that individuals, regardless of age or background, could prepare themselves for employment—for a career. States were to be assisted in developing or expanding state scholarship plans, again to encourage equality of opportunity. Institutions were to be assisted in developing programs to help returning veterans achieve rather than fail. Postsecondary education was to be improved through a new governmental unit giving emphasis to experimentation and innovation. Research was to be given impetus and status. An Assistant Secretary of Education was to be appointed to provide leadership and coordinate this great new package of enlightened legislation, the Education Amendments of 1972. Higher education—postsecondary education—was to become a reality for those who desired it and who could profit from what it had to offer. The breakthrough had come for students and institutions alike. The federal and state governments would join hands in helping to assist the different types of institutions, public, private, or proprietary, whether academically or occupationally oriented, whether large or small, rural or urban—for this diversity would be required if students with pluralistic needs were to be served with efficient and high quality educational programs.

These and other sections of the Amendments made a package which if fully funded would have cost approximately five billion dollars—close to the total Office of Education budget for fiscal 1972. There was an awareness that this was too large an amount to be funded for fiscal 1974, so priorities had to be established. The overwhelming issue was who should establish the priorities? The higher education community asked for almost four billion dollars, which sum included provision for all sections of the Amendments with the exception of two: emergency assistance and facility aid. The Administration countered with an offer of some 1.7 billion dollars, which included 959 million for the Basic Education Opportunity Grants, 250 million for college work-study, 310 million for the Guaranteed Student Loan Program, 70 million for the Trio Program, 100 million for developing institutions, 15 million for the improvement of postsecondary education, and little else. The emphasis of the Administration was on student assistance, especially assistance to students from low-income families. Other elements of the Amendments considered very important by educational institutions, by Congress, and by many administration spokesmen were not recommended for funding because of the 250 billion dollar limitation placed on the fiscal 1973 budget and the 269 billion dollar limitation placed on the fiscal 1974 budget.

The higher education community reacted this time with a set of priorities which totaled much less than their original request, but which were well in excess of the Administration's position. No action has been taken by Congress at this time concerning either the fiscal 1973 or 1974 budgets. In the meantime, students and institutions alike are worried and confused as to what will be approved in the way of aid to those concerned. There are no present answers, only conjectures. Confusion and frustration reign, and time is running out.

A presidentially appointed National Commission to Study the Financing of Postsecondary Education is functioning, but its report will not be presented until December 1973. Other groups such as the Committee on Economic Development, the Carnegie Commission, a group brought together by the Sloan Foundation (from Yale University, Duke University, and the Ten College Group), are studying, experimenting, and recommending possible courses of action to help solve the financial concerns of both students and institutions. The concerns are serious, and the need to reach agreements and to initiate action is urgent.

Complicating the situation facing higher education in the coming years is the use of the term postsecondary education throughout the Education Amendments. As noted earlier, it is emphasized in the language establishing state planning commissions, the national commission on financing, and in the improvement of postsecondary education. Technical Institutes, proprietary institutions, and other types of teaching and learning institutions are to be included in the planning and investigations now being initiated. Like it or not, the higher education world of two- and four-year colleges and universities has been drastically altered. In numbers of institutions alone, the figure has grown to approximately seven thousand, with some type of acceptable accreditation. If the unaccredited institutions were to be included, the number would increase to perhaps twelve thousand—if it were possible to identify them since these tend to proliferate like rabbits and die like lemmings.

The postsecondary turf has indeed been changed, and there is confusion, hope and fear with respect to finding, and reaching agreement on, an acceptable definition. The definition must be acceptable to the Congress which passed the legislation, to the Administration which approved it, and especially to the students, institutions, and taxpayers who will have to live with it. Proposed definitions include any public or private institution which offers instruction beyond the secondary level, or enrolls students eighteen years of age or older who can profit from the educational offerings. This definition is similar to that used by many of the comprehensive community colleges. In addition, proprietary institutions and technical institutes enrolling groups at similar levels and ages will be included. Educational offerings by the armed forces, veterans organizations, business and industry, labor, and home-study programs have been recommended for inclusion, as has the non-traditional learning and evaluation of learning through the granting of credits towards an external degree. In other words, the emphasis will be on what is learned beyond secondary education or the age of eighteen, rather than on the higher education institution as traditionally defined by the regional accrediting associations. This is revolutionary in concept, and, as is the case with all revolutions, must be watched with caution and objective evaluation. If the federal government is to provide students with financial assistance when they participate in such programs, care must be taken with respect to the quality and integrity of the programs. Fiascos occurred when the con artists vicimized veterans and the government after the second world war. This must not be permitted to recur.

The higher education community, in cooperation with representatives of those institutions not previously included in the traditional definition, must plan to be sure that students with their pluralisic needs are provided with quality educational offerings. A great diversity of institutions and learning methods probably will be included in the definition of postsecondary education.

It is of the utmost importance that each type of institution, public, private, or proprietary, have clearly stated objectives and that the institutions adhere to the stated objectives. Only through such clarity of purpose and adherence to it can a particular institution, and the much needed diversity of institutions, be maintained and, it is hoped, expanded. It would indeed be a tragedy if institutions were to drift into a homogeneous state through their emulation of one another. The great public and private universities, the private liberal arts colleges, the state colleges, the community colleges, the technical institutes, the business, industry, and labor schools, the armed forces, all and each have their own purposes and strengths. These are weakened when such institutions attempt to expand beyond their qualifications. A university is seldom able to serve well the occupational training function of a community college. A state college cannot provide the scholarly research demanded in the graduate programs of a university. A technical institute is not equipped to duplicate the offerings of a liberal arts college. Each type has its responsibilities to the students it serves, and its status is measured by the quality of the appropriate service it provides. Status should not, and cannot, be achieved through an inadequate and inferior emulation of a different type of institution, nor should the states or federal government provide material or philosophi-

cal support for such emulation. Unneeded and indefensible duplication of effort must be eliminated where it exists, and prevented from
occurring where it is proposed—both within states and in regions
which overlap state boundaries.

We who are concerned professionally must be deeply involved
in the planning and decision-making process. Our absence has been
noted by both the legislative and administrative branches of government. We have not provided either with the facts or with unbiased,
objective recommendations. We have tended to go our own way, pro-
ceeding unilaterally too often at the expense of the other segments
of higher or postsecondary education. The dearth of knowledge in the
legislative and administrative branches of government about higher,
or post-secondary education, and the dearth of knowledge among professional educators about the totality of higher or post-secondary education is causing decisions to be made from ignorance which in the
long run may well change our lives, and the lives of our students, in a
negative and perhaps destructive manner. This ignorance is too often
combined with arrogance in an unholy alliance, and we, the professionals, and the students are the victims. However, the responsibility
and the blame, if there is blame, must rest with us. We should assume
the leadership for planning tomorrow's postsecondary educational programs. We should provide the facts upon which legislators create policy. We should educate the members of the executive branches of government about the needs and realities of our programs and institutions.
Through our naivete and disinclination to participate actively in the
decision-making processes of government, we have encouraged and
permitted others with strong biases, but little knowledge of the issues,
to make the decisions which regulate our institutions, and the lives
and hopes of millions of students. Both our neglect of the obligation
to be aware and the arrogance of the biased decision-maker are indefensible from any view point.

We have agreed that our citizens, regardless of age, race, or
economic background have a right to postsecondary education. We
have agreed that the equality of opportunity to strive for something
better—culturally, socially or economically—is the right of all of our
people. We have agreed that equal access to institutions by students
who are qualified for admission to such institutions—regardless of their
affluence or lack of affluence—is a goal of this country, and one that
can be partially provided for through the entitlement concept of the
Educational Amendments of 1972.

Congress has legislated, and the President has approved the legislation which establishes the broader concept of postsecondary education as the vehicle by which these goals and agreements can and will be realized. I hope we have reached that degree of maturity in which we are ready to believe that each person's achievement will enrich that person and hence will enrich each one of us and society as a whole.

22

The Education
Amendments and
the Future

Roger W. Heyns

Dramatic questions are posed by President Nixon's program for education, regarding both the role and amount of federal participation in domestic programs and the form of that participation. As for the mode or form of participation, the President's program appears to have two interrelated but distinguishable parts: funding in large categories, and increased discretionary authority at the state and local levels. In those areas in which there should be federal participation, the President has said that the categories of support should be broad, and discretion at the local level should be substantial, through both general and specific revenue sharing. These are indubitably popular ideas with the public at large. In the interests of candor, I should acknowledge that the decentralization and freedom from federal controls that are an inevitable effect of narrow categorical programs have been popular ideas in both the liberal and conservative segments of the academic community.

One might properly have reservations about the promiscuity of the approach, remembering that many of the programs presently supported by the federal government and now proposed for decentralization arose originally out of neglect, or out of the inability of state and local government to meet the needs. One must also register one's fear, based on reasonable grounds, that the groups most likely to suffer in any priority discussion at the local level are the poor and the ethnic minorities. Nevertheless, these are empirical issues and not matters of principle. While I want to describe the general situation as objectively as possible, I do not wish to imply complete agreement with the President's program, or to suggest a flagging of my interest in getting the Congress to improve the program of support for education.

We, as a nation, are being required by the President's budget to reconsider the role of the federal government and its relation to state and regional government. It does not seem to me to be a partisan statement that the issue is a proper one; it has been clearly stated and it now behooves us to engage in the analytical task of determining answers to such questions as where this new posture is appropriate and where it is not, what kinds of monitoring are required of the federal government, what guidelines are needed in what areas, and, finally, what are the appropriate mechanisms for decision making at the state and local levels?

Turning next to the question of amount of federal participation, it is clear that here again the President has strong public support for reduced federal spending, and the academic community is not different from the general public in its concern with controlling inflation. But apart from reduced federal spending as a part of fiscal policy, there is the larger question of the discrepancy between authorized programs and expenditure levels for those programs. This gap has been growing steadily for years now. Elliott Richardson, when he was Secretary of HEW, observed in a speech given to HEW employees in December 1971: "In the first full budget of the Kennedy administration, congressional authorizations for HEW programs exceeded amounts requested for their operation by $200 million. In the current fiscal year, authorizations for HEW programs exceed appropriations by $6 billion. Legislation likely to be enacted by this Congress may add still another $9 billion in new authorizations for next year and even larger amounts for future years."

This discrepancy between our revenue and our national domestic goals, as represented in legislation passed by Congress and signed by the Chief Executive, is now staggering; the current Presidential budget enlarges it, but it does not create it.

There are theoretically two ways to close the gap between our goals and our current ability to support them. One is to change our goals, lowering some and eliminating others. The other is to increase our revenue. It is clear that no substantial segment of either party is seriously interested in this latter possibility. While there is considerable talk of tax reform, it deals primarily with loopholes and inequities, whether real or alleged. No politician is proposing an increase in taxation; on the contrary, even the reformers do not propose an overall increase in federal revenue. Nor do I think this reluctance is likely to change in the near future. There is too much general dissatisfaction with present programs or uncertainty about their effectiveness. This uncertainty is widespread—in the Congress, in the executive branch, and in the public at large—and it covers almost the entire sweep of federal programs: education, agriculture, literacy, housing, transportation, urban problems, and welfare. Education is not a particular target.

What is going to come out of this? Predictably, understandably, and justifiably, the interested parties in all these areas will shout long and loudly. The general decibel level will drown out and render ineffective the shouts from all but a few areas. However, I hope that the outcome will be a serious examination of each of the programs, a well-documented analysis of the consequences of certain levels of funding, and an assessment of the relative priorities among these programs. Such a massive reevaluation of our national aspirations is inevitable and imperative. It is also to be hoped that Congress will facilitate this process by organizing itself so that it can assess the cumulative impact of what are now segmental choices.

But it is not Congress alone for whom there is a message in the massive debate and reappraisal that lies before us. We in education must develop a new style and new habits. Up until very recently, our posture has been to identify a need and satisfy others that it existed. After the program to meet the need was established, we asked for annual increments and usually, largely on the basis of efforts by friends of education in the administration and both houses of Congress, the increments came. We were riding along on the general momentum to which so much attention is now being called. Now, if we are to participate effectively, and in the interest of the nation, in this reappraisal of national goals, we must be prepared to demonstrate, as clearly as possible, the consequences in human terms of various levels and forms of funding. We must work harder than ever at appraising the effectiveness of what we do. I am not suggesting that the problem of measuring the outputs of education is an easy one. Nor do I believe that we should be diffident about claiming, as benefits of postsecondary training, outcomes that are difficult to assess. Education is not alone among human enterprises that have more or less intangible effects. These activities persist with society's support because there is a collective wisdom—an intuitive sense—that they are valuable. Having said this, however, I believe we must increase our efforts to assess the effectiveness of our curricula and our pedagogical methods. We must be prepared to defend the choices we make and we must commit ourselves to demonstrating a relationship between the methods we use and the outcomes we seek. In addition to this hardheaded appraisal of our effectiveness we must be prepared to make choices, to assign high priority to certain of our needs and lower priority to others. It is unrealistic, at the present time, to think that we will succeed in persuading the Congress and the administration, or state and local governments, for that matter, to support all the existing programs and all the proposed new ones. To adopt that posture would be to claim a unique place among the social programs of the nation and to insist on a special exemption for ourselves from the common requirement. Paranoia on our part—the belief that we have been singled out for mistreatment—is not warranted.

It is in this context that I turn to describing the educational landscape in the light of the higher education amendments. The 1972 amendments have recognized, by legislative means, groups of institutions which up to now have not been eligible for federal support programs, and they have extended the participation of other types of institutions that had already been eligible for some programs. More important, in the stimulation toward planning at the state level represented by the 1202 section, passed by the Congress and signed by the executive, the federal government asserted the importance of representation of the interests of these new groups. The situation is made slightly ambiguous by the fact that guidelines for the 1202 Commissions will not be issued and the Commissions will not be funded, but my view is that the trend has been established toward greater participation by junior and community colleges, by proprietary schools, and by vocational and technical schools in the planning process at the state level. This trend will not be reversed by the temporary halt on the process of establishing 1202 Commissions. Finally, we should not ignore the fact that in the history of the legislation and in the amendments themselves there is reflected an interest in and concern for private education.

All of this is to say that the scope of postsecondary education has been enlarged. This is an exciting and valuable development, with all sorts of potential for good administration and a number of challenges and risks.

But, before I begin a discussion of some of the implications, let me observe that the primary motivation for the creation of an enlarged community of post-secondary education comes from the Congress and the executive branch. As Joseph Cosand pointed out in the preceding essay, there was widespread participation in the amendments by educators. The idea that all of us are engaged in a common enterprise—the education of the young beyond the high school—and must work together for the common good came from the society, as represented in the Congress and the Executive.

Now our task is to give full implementation to this mandate of creating an effective community of diverse educational institutions, serving different student populations with different objectives. And this task puts a dialectic in process that would delight Hegel. We must pursue two goals simultaneously that will tax the wisdom and maturity of all of us.

The first is to strengthen our habits of working together, as institutions and as associations, toward those objectives of education which we have in common—through the pooling of resources, when that is desirable, and through eliminating duplication. We must engage in joint political and public education efforts to secure for postsecondary education the support that it needs to do the tasks assigned to it. We must reinforce each other in the constant effort toward high quality education in all its forms. We must implement the national commitment to provide educational opportunity for all, and particularly we must accelerate the rate at which ethnic minorities and women are represented in all phases of education. These are but a few of the many common tasks and we must work strenuously at them.

The other goal is to maintain diversity. The pressures of the common tasks in the new situation will bring us together; but we should resist the subtle pressures of being included in common support programs and the not-so-subtle pressures of there being increasingly limited sources of funds that could result in our becoming more alike. Our commitment to diversity will be sorely tested.

Yet the health of individual institutions and of the system as a whole seems to me to rest upon a common commitment to diversiy. We must encourage each of our diverse types of institutions in their efforts to define for themselves their distinctive role. A healthy diversity can only be achieved if institutions are obliged to define their educational goals clearly and in such a way as to differentiate themselves from others. The same clarity and differentiation are required with respect to defining the clientele the institution intends to serve, and the climate for learning it intends to create to meet those goals for its clientele. Our dependence on enrollment and on providing educational opportunities in order to obtain support have increased the tendency to be all things to all men and women. With a real sense of the entire system, with a recognition of the need for diverse parts, we can reduce these pressures. And with purposes and procedures and clientele clearly defined, it will be possible for students to make appropriate choices. This process of definition will inevitably produce a better fit between the institution's aims and its resources, human, physical, and financial.

Educational institutions live with a very high level of self-induced frustration. Quite properly, our goals exceed our grasp. We want more student aid, greater educational opportunity for the heretofore deprived, better materials and equipment, higher salaries, smaller classrooms, more programs for students to choose among, and bigger and better libraries. And in my experience, these aspirations have not been self-seeking in the sense that the individuals making the demands on the part of institutions are themselves likely to profit personally if these goals are attained. Yet, I believe that it is in our collective interest to reduce the level of self-induced frustration by means of this better fit I have described. It is preferable, I am arguing, that some have good conditions in which to live, work, and learn, than for all to have a dead level of gloom and inadequacy, and a discrepancy between aims and the capacity to achieve them that is barely tolerable or insupportable. This "fitting" of goals, clientele, pedagogical method, and resources will not only reduce this self-imposed frustration but it will also increase our diversity.

But the maintenance of useful, valid diversity is not merely, or even primarily, a matter of organizational arrangements, or the intellectual awareness of the desirability of diversity, or the arrangements for allocating the common resources. An important ingredient in our success in achieving this diverse community is our attitude toward all postsecondary education tasks. We have operated with a limited set of models and these models have been ordered into a prestige hierarchy in subtle and not-so-subtle ways. We have all seen some junior and community colleges put a disproportionate share of their resources into college transfer programs to the neglect of their vocational and technical training tasks. We have seen products of graduate schools influenced, during their graduate training, to limiting their employment aspirations to institutions that most closely resembled their own graduate schools. We have seen pressures toward activities of high prestige, such as graduate training and research, distort the integrity of institutions, strain their resources and reduce their effectiveness with their other tasks.

Much of this is our own doing—reflections of our attitudes, our own snobbery. Only if we can embrace, with conviction and respect, a range of educational tasks, a large variety of educational settings, and the partnership of fellow teachers with quite different skills than our own, will we enhance the diversity we need and secure the community we seek. In our newly awakened concern for the nontraditional, the vocational and the technical, and for the proprietary institutions, we must not now demean the absolutely essential activities of the large research or graduate training institutions. They, in turn, must not in their current embattled state derogate the newly enfranchised. And all the other types must develop those same feelings of mutual respect.

These are our tasks, then, for the future: To create a community—a genuine voluntary system of postsecondary education through the sharing of common tasks—and to preserve and strengthen within that community a healthy diversity.

Index

205